BREAKING THE MOLD

Women, Men, and Time
in the New Corporate World

Lotte Bailyn

THE FREE PRESS
A Division of Macmillan, Inc.
NEW YORK

Maxwell Macmillan Canada
TORONTO

Maxwell Macmillan International
NEW YORK   OXFORD   SINGAPORE   SYDNEY

The Free Press
A Division of Macmillan, Inc.
866 Third Avenue, New York, N.Y. 10022

Maxwell Macmillan Canada, Inc.
1200 Eglinton Avenue East
Suite 200
Don Mills, Ontario M3C 3N1

Macmillan, Inc. is part of the Maxwell Communication
Group of Companies.

Printed in the United States of America

printing number
1 2 3 4 5 6 7 8 9 10

Library of Congress Cataloging-in-Publication Data

Bailyn, Lotte.
    Breaking the mold : women, men, and time in the new corporate
world / Lotte Bailyn.
        p. cm.
    Includes bibliographical references and index.
    ISBN 0-02-901281-3
    1. Work and family—United States.   2. Industry—Social aspects—
United States.   I. Title.
    HD4904.25.B33   1993
    306.3'6—dc20   93-25795
                                                                CIP

The author is grateful to the publishers listed here for permission to use excerpts from her previous works, adapted for the present book.

"Resolving Contradictions in Technical Careers." Reprinted with permission from *Technology Review*, copyright © 1982.

"The Hybrid Career: An Exploratory Study of Career Routes in R & D." Reprinted with permission from *Journal of Engineering and Technology Management* (1991).

"Changing the Conditions of Work: Responding to Increasing Work Force Diversity and New Family Patterns." From *Transforming Organizations,* edited by Thomas A. Kochan and Michael Useem. Copyright © 1992 by The Sloan School of Management. Reprinted by permission of Oxford University Press, Inc.

"Issues of Work and Family in Different National Contexts: How the U.S., Britain and Sweden Respond." Reprinted with permission from *Human Resource Management,* copyright © 1992 by John Wiley & Sons, Inc.

"Freeing Work from the Constraints of Location and Time." From *New Technology, Work and Employment* 3 (1988). Reprinted by permission of Blackwell Publishers.

"Patterned Chaos in Human Resource Management." Reprinted from *Sloan Management Review* 34 (Winter 1993), pp. 77–78 and 81, by permission of the publisher. Copyright © 1993 by the Sloan Management Review Association. All rights reserved.

To Mitzi
and to Charles and John

CONTENTS

Preface

These early studies, done mainly in the 1970s and the first half of the 1980s, dealt primarily with male employees whose wives provided family support—the "traditional" employees of the industrial age. Since that time, however, a new situation has developed. Partly because of economic changes both globally and in the United States, partly because of the consequences of political developments in the last decade, and partly because of dramatic demographic shifts in the work force, a new set of problems has appeared, which have come to be known as issues of work and family. These problems seemed to me equal in importance to those I had been studying previously and to intersect with them in complicated and significant ways.

And so I put off writing the book I had planned and proceeded to study these developing issues. I turned to the concerns of women, who were now more frequently entering the technical work force, and compared their career experiences with those of technically trained men. I also studied the phenomenon of telecommuting—working at home on high-level tasks (often with a computer) instead of commuting to a central office location. I took a close look at managers ten years into their careers to see how they were dealing with the joint issues of their careers and their personal lives. And, with a number of colleagues and the support of the Ford Foundation, I started intensive study of one large and successful organization to probe the possibility of reconfiguring work to deal with these issues.

I soon discovered a central problem. Responding to the growing concern about American competitiveness, companies are attempting to develop what they hope will be more productive ways of organizing work, using total quality management, empowerment, self-managed teams, and fewer management levels. The essence of these proposed changes lies in intensifying employees' involvement with their organizations, not by the simple exchange of work for pay but through broader participation and the sharing of goals. While certain aspects of these new ways of organizing work are congruent with emerging personal needs, others create problems. In particular, the increased in-

volvement demanded by these new arrangements requires more
time and energy from employees than they can easily provide
given the increasingly complicated pressures of their private lives.
The difficult cross-pressures that result can only be resolved by
new ways of relating employment to the needs of families. The
separation of these domains in the traditional organization of
work is no longer tenable. Public and private spheres must now
be linked, and the conditions of employment must be reconsidered.

The background of these issues is not unfamiliar. There is
general recognition that society is changing in fundamental
ways. Companies are aware that more women are in the work
force, that there is a significant number of employed single parents, and that the career goals and expectations of employees, especially technical and professional workers, are shifting. It is also
known that intensified work commitment puts the care of dependents at risk and reduces involvement with community and
leisure activities.

Some companies have attempted to respond to these
changes by providing child care, family leave, and flexible work
arrangements. But these responses do not confront the critical
issue of how best to organize work in this new world. Presented
as solutions at the margin, they are not always successful. Men
prove to be unwilling to take advantage of flexible arrangements
when offered and reluctant to take time off when it is
labeled paternity leave. Women continue to have primary responsibility for the "second shift"—the work of the home—even
when fully engaged in paid employment. Managers, moreover,
continue to find it difficult to relinquish continuous visual over-
sight of their employees.

Behind these problems lie deeply seated, central assumptions about work and control. Managers are expected to control
the work, and employees are presumed to have no responsibilities other than to their companies. This view of employment
stems from a gendered construction of the separation of spheres:
the view that compensated work (involvement in the public
sphere) is the province of men and quite separate from involve-

ment in the home, which is deemed the particular and appropriate concern of women.

A reconsideration of this separation of public and private life, and the changes in the organization of work that such a rethinking requires, have emerged as the central themes of this book. I look at these problems from the point of view of both employers and employees, and I address the people who are personally involved in these issues as well as the colleagues and supervisors whose work must be coordinated with theirs.

The analysis is based on the conviction that it is possible simultaneously to meet the productivity needs of American companies *and* the personal needs of their employees, and that to emphasize only one of these critical concerns will necessarily undermine the other. Moreover, I submit that these are not peripheral issues that can be left to personnel assistants and counselors. On the contrary, they lie at the core of the challenges facing American industry. There is no escape from these problems; companies *must* include—explicitly, imaginatively, and effectively—the private needs of employees when reengineering their work. Only if they do so can they gain a competitive edge.

The story in the chapters that follow is anchored in extensive empirical research. It presents, in generally accessible form, an analysis and interpretation of more than two decades of detailed studies of technical, professional, and managerial employees. I am aware, of course, that this group represents only a minority of American workers, but it is an influential and in many ways powerful minority. Other groups in this country, without the educational or economic advantages of the people I have studied, have never had the luxury of "traditional" family life and have always had to improvise bridges between public and private worlds, often with great difficulty. Their stories must also be told, and slowly they are being told as scholars turn to a deeper understanding of privilege and deprivation in American society. This book, however, concentrates on people in technical, professional, and managerial positions, who play distinctive roles in American economic life.

Preface

Though empirically based, this book is also in part a personal story. I have been involved with these problems personally as well as professionally for several decades during which changes in circumstances and in social views have been dramatic. The research I have done has reflected my personal attempt to come to terms with these issues and with the ways they have been approached. I am part of a generation of educated women who had it both harder and easier than our successors. We had to struggle against overt discrimination that for the most part no longer exists, but we also were available when the world began to change and was actively seeking qualified women.

The difficulties are now more subtle, and they are no longer confined to women; they affect all employees in high-level occupational roles. The assumption that work roles can engage the exclusive commitment of those who occupy them is no longer tenable. Nor can the difficulties of pursuing complex careers any longer be seen as individual dilemmas, to be solved in isolation. The issues transcend individual boundaries. They involve the very core of organizational processes and demand dramatic revision in a number of key underlying assumptions of organizational life.

I do not present in what follows a detailed blueprint for effecting necessary change. Nor do I think that there is necessarily any "best practice" in this complicated area. My aim is to identify and analyze the key issues that need rethinking, to define the problems and consider useful approaches to them. My hope is to assist employers and employees jointly in finding ways to accommodate both the competitive needs of the company and the personal concerns of the individual worker in a manner consistent with their particular circumstances. Taken by themselves, such accommodations, while necessary, will not be sufficient; ultimately they will have to be buttressed by social and cultural reinforcement. But I see such changes within organizations as crucial first steps if the responses to these emerging and increasingly difficult problems are to be systemic rather than idiosyncratic, dealing with only one issue and sacrificing other important goals.

Preface

* * *

Many people have contributed to my thinking on these questions. My colleagues at MIT, Edgar H. Schein and John Van Maanen, have always been supportive of my work, and over the years I have learned much from having to come to terms with their different views of the world. I am also grateful to Ed Schein for his suggestions on an earlier draft of this book.

The input of Deborah Kolb, who also read a draft, has been extraordinarily helpful, even though I was not able to meet all her goals. She and Rhona Rapoport have been long-standing colleagues and friends whose influence on my thinking has been profound. Almost twenty-five years ago, Rhona Rapoport provided me with the first opportunity to investigate some of these concerns empirically, and continues to be a valuable consultant to that work. She also introduced me to June Zeitlin of the Ford Foundation, who has supported my most recent research studies.

The research team with whom I am currently studying this topic in one eminently successful company has proved an endless source of insight and delight. Besides Deborah Kolb, the team includes Amy Andrews, Joyce Fletcher, Maureen Harvey, Robin Johnson, and Leslie Perlow, all of whom have expanded my understanding and appreciation of the complexity of these issues. I would also like to express appreciation to the employees in that company who have collaborated with us in this endeavor.

Lori Pavadore has shared her industrial experience with me, and I have benefited from many conversations with Michael B. Arthur. I am grateful also to Dalia Etzion and Constance Perin for collaboration on earlier research projects. And I thank Susan McLean for her tireless help in producing the many revisions of the chapters in this book, and Patricia Robinson for assistance in tracking down references.

I am grateful, too, to Susan Arellano of The Free Press, whose patience and perceptiveness throughout the revisions of this book have been of great help. And I thank Jill Kneerim for getting me in touch with her. Edith Lewis of The Free Press has also been most helpful.

Preface

Marie Jahoda Albu has always supported my work, sometimes almost too uncritically. In contrast, Bernard Bailyn has been my greatest critic as well as my greatest supporter. I thank him for his efforts in both roles. Needless to say, both of these supporters have had a profound effect on my life. Finally, Charles and John have not supported this work in any way, but their presence makes it all worthwhile.

CHAPTER 1

INTRODUCTION
The World We Live In

S ix men, employees of a large and successful manufacturing company, were sitting around a table. They had come together to discuss the findings of a study on the relation between family and work among the company's employees. Three of them were in their fifties and had worked for the company for twenty to thirty years; they dominated the conversation. One, Nathan Glass,* was particularly indignant:

> I don't think the company should have anything to say about a person's family. Everyone must choose. If they want to have children, then the wife better stay home to care for them. And

---

*The names used in examples throughout this book are pseudonyms, but the facts are all true.

if they want the extra income in order to indulge themselves, they better not have children. It's simply a matter of choice.

The three younger men stayed silent, but their lives represented a very different reality. One was an engineer whose wife had a successful career of her own. They were expecting to have children, and he wanted to make sure that the company would give him paternity leave at the birth of his child. He was willing to take it as unpaid leave, but he could not afford (nor did he want) to sacrifice his job. Another, a young technician, wondered whether he and his girlfriend would ever be able to afford a house, and whether they could even consider the possibility of having children.

To the younger men, Nathan's pronouncement came from a world they did not know: a world where one income could support a family, where men spent all their time and energy generating that income, and where women made it all possible by using their time and energy—without material reward—to take care of the rest of life. It was a world where the public sphere of economic activity was quite separate from the private arena of family care; a world in which companies could presume that their employees had no responsibilities outside of their paid work.

Despite the unreality of this image to the younger men, the company they worked for still functioned as if the lives of its employees fit this picture of the world. Corporate practices anchored in this traditional mold seemed unproblematic in the day of *The Organization Man*, "Leave It to Beaver," and *The Feminine Mystique*, but the world has changed dramatically since then. To give just one example, in 1960 fewer than one in five married mothers with children under six was in the work force; in the early 1990s more than three in five are.

To break this outdated mold, and to make companies more responsive to the needs of the current work force, we must question and reevaluate some key beliefs. Why are professional employees expected to work such long hours? Can one really accomplish more in twelve hours than in ten, or eight? Some evidence, to be discussed in a later chapter, clearly indicates that the answer is no. And why is visibility—presence at the workplace—such a critical indicator of commitment? Many tasks, particularly those that require careful thought and attention, are accomplished better and more easily away from an office. Again, the evidence is available, though it has not been assimilated into our underlying beliefs. Are there not other, perhaps better ways of working that could build on this evidence? Can we imagine a world where work is shared among more people, thus reducing extremes of both underemployment and overwork?

Much is possible, but only if organizations give the private needs and concerns of their employees a legitimate place in the planning of work. These personal issues must take a central role as business objectives; they cannot be relegated to the margins without negative repercussions for both employees and their employers. What is needed is a different way of thinking about employees—not as workers only but as people with complicated lives for whom employment is a critical, but not the only, activity—and an acceptance of the necessary link between their private lives and the work of the organization.

In arguing for greater integration between people's public and private lives, I do not subscribe to a "work hard/play hard" model similar to Japan, where the organization co-opts private time and private emotions for the employer. In such suggestions the "line between public and private becomes fuzzy,"[1] but in only one direction. Nor do I mean to imply that an organization should shift from one set of assumptions to their exact opposites. There will always be people whose personal needs are fully involved with their work. The key challenge, therefore, is for companies to find ways of dealing with a heterogeneous work force. They need to get away from uniform and monolithic expectations, and to move toward multiplicity and pluralism. If they do, they may discover different and unexpectedly more effective ways of reaching their goals.

We know, for example, that the family's involvement with schools is very important to the education of the next generation, and we know that America's competitive position is dependent on an educated work force. So with the number of dual-career and single-parent families increasing, we have to confront the question of how parents working in an environment of doing more with less, which necessarily implies the "need to sacrifice some personal time,"[2] can find the time or energy to get involved in their children's schools. If companies were to provide time for parents to visit schools and meet with teachers, might not then a number of important objectives be reached simultaneously? But for companies to do so would require a new way of thinking about their employees.

Current conditions challenge the assumption, held for most of this century, that the public world of political and economic activity is and should be distinct from the private domain of relationships and care.[3] Though it has been assumed that the two arenas are guided by different values and standards—and are controlled by a different sex—demographic changes and new values and life-styles call for greater integration between the two spheres. Advances in information and communication technology provide a vehicle for potentially bridging the divide. Modern organizations, however, find it difficult to respond to these changing circumstances in the work force because the rest of their world is in such flux. Pressures from global competition seem to call for even greater effort from employees, and a plea for more flexible accommodation to personal needs seems peculiarly out of place.

It is the thesis of this book, however, that framing the issue as a conflict between employees' private needs and the competitive and productivity needs of American enterprise is self-defeating for both. I hope to provide a different way of thinking about the link between public and private life that will allow the work of American companies to be organized to create synergy rather than conflict between these two spheres. The goal is to break the mold of traditional assumptions; the hope is that the needs of organizations and employees can be brought into a constructive harmony.

CONTOURS OF THE PROBLEM

Most of us would agree with Freud that *lieben* and *arbeiten* (love and work) are the keys to a mature personality. We want both, and yet we often find it difficult to have both. We do not confront an entirely new problem, therefore, but one that is of particular urgency at this time because of changes in our country: demographic changes and changes in attitudes and values.

Cycles in the birthrate, differential age distributions and fertility rates among different groups of people, and new patterns of immigration are all altering the U.S. population mix. As a whole, the American population is expected to age by the year 2000, with the result that there may be a scarcity of people to fill entry-level positions. And though there is some question about whether the nation will face an actual labor shortage at that time, it seems clear that the profile of the labor force will be different from what it is now.

Further, the participation of women in paid work is projected to continue to rise further than that of men (which may actually decline). The group with the highest rate of growth and the greatest increase in its contribution to the labor force in this final decade of the century is expected to be women in their prime working years. And since women are now a majority in the college population, their skills may turn out to be critical for the future work force.[4]

The makeup of the family and the distribution of types of households are also becoming noticeably different from what they have been. Since about the middle 1970s, there have been more dual-worker than "traditional" families in the United States. Three-quarters of families with children are headed by married couples, and of these, nearly two-thirds have both parents in the labor force.[5] Moreover, the rise in the divorce rate and in children out of wedlock has led to an increasing number of single-parent households, the preponderance of which are headed by women.

All of these developments put great pressure on family care, but so far there has been little institutional response in this area. U.S. national policy, through social security, unemployment, and disability provisions, has been mainly concerned with ensuring support for periods of disengagement from paid work. Employers and unions for much of the last fifty years have been primarily interested in a family wage, an earning level sufficient for a single breadwinner to support a family. And standard company benefits, which have grown dramatically since the end of World War II, have similarly been mainly geared to the needs of a male-supported family. Only recently, since two-earner families have become the norm, have some companies begun to deal with the ensuing issues through more innovative and flexible benefit packages.[6] But in the last quarter century the American family has been transformed. So, as Levitan and Conway suggest, instead of a family wage, what may now be necessary is a *family workweek* in order to enable parents to have a better balance between work and family responsibilities.[7]

The demographic changes noted above are among those that have contributed to the issues explored in this book. They have been accompanied also—and are interrelated with—changes in attitudes and values of the American people about what is important in their lives. A first indication of these changes came from researchers at AT & T who had been following the careers of a cohort of managers since the early 1950s. Two decades into this work, when they decided to start a fresh cohort, the researchers discovered significant differences in attitudes. What surprised them was that the younger cohort did not seem to have the same ambitions and eagerness to get ahead that had been the hallmark of the successful managers who started their careers in the immediate postwar period.[8]

Similarly, Leinberger and Tucker studied the sons and daughters of the men interviewed by William H. Whyte in *The Organization Man,* and found their values to be very different. They were well educated, autonomous, antihierarchical, much less competitive and more cooperative than their fathers, and "pouring more psychic energy into family and community" than their fathers had done: "But it is not that they do not want to work. They want to work differently. They want a new balance in their compact with the organization and they will walk if they don't get it."[9] They represent a better-educated work force, with many of the characteristics needed for the shift from an industrial world based on principles of scientific management[10] to one centered on information and on abilities of conceptualization and abstraction. But their interests in work seem to be more related to self-worth than to material ends.[11]

Today most of the leaders and top managers of American enterprises are still in the old mold, and their presence reinforces traditional procedures. In 1988, for example, only a few members of the younger generation were leaders of top companies.[12] Over the next two decades, however, the present leaders will retire, and the new generation will move into their ranks. Combined with other developments, this change in outlook among those setting policy may precipitate changes that will make it easier for an increasingly diverse work force to contribute to the American economy without sacrificing the demands of family and community.

A key question is how the organizational innovations being developed in order to meet America's competitive needs mesh with the changing desires and interests of individual employees and their families. Many of the characteristics of the "transformed" organization conform to the needs and concerns of the newer generations. Kanter describes the "post-entrepreneurial revolution" as one in which employees' careers shift "from climbing to hopping."[13] Since recent trends toward restructuring and downsizing have in any case made workers' loyalty to their employers looser, this mode fits current conditions. And the shifting nature of work toward more accountability and responsibility at the working level also meshes with this generation's greater interest in task than in position.

But there are personal costs to these new forms. Most involve an implicit exchange between greater autonomy and challenge on the one hand and 110 percent effort, or the "need to sacrifice some personal time," on the other.[14] Such "requirements" introduce personal stress and exacerbate the pressures on family care already heightened by demographic changes. Some of the problem centers on time; the notion of a "family workweek" does not characteristically enter companies' policies or figure in the writings on the needs of American business.[15] But the legitimacy of personal concerns is probably a more critical point: A highly influential report on American productivity, for example, with a heavy emphasis on the development of human resources, does not even have the word *family* in the index.[16]

The lack of integration of public and private spheres is more evident in this country than in many other Western industrialized nations. A recent attempt to compare the United States with Canada and the European Community on these issues concluded that Americans, on average, pay lower taxes and have a higher standard of living than inhabitants of these other countries, but they do so at some cost.[17] One clear cost is the polarization of U.S. society into those who benefit from this standard of living and those who do not. But all employed Americans pay for their "advantage" by longer working hours and fewer government benefits. Employees in Western Europe have more paid holidays and vacation days, and flexible working conditions such as flextime are more prevalent there than they are in the United States. And, the analysis concluded, the higher expenditure of these countries on social benefits does not seem to affect their economies adversely.

In the absence of government support on behalf of families, leading American companies have introduced a variety of programs designed to deal with issues of diversity and family need. But diversity, characteristically, has been taken to mean concern for women and minorities; work and family issues have been defined as relevant only to female employees. One management consultant, when asked to comment on work and family issues at his company, replied that "work/family is not an issue because there are no women in this firm." And in response to an attempt by one large company to elicit its employees' views of work-family issues, "traditional" employees translated the question into an inquiry about the company's affirmative action effort and expressed dismay at the "very limited upward mobility for white males."

These issues are obviously *not* limited to women and minorities. The changes described above affect all employees. Organizations that respond only in terms of the "nontraditional" worker risk backlash and confusion. White males, as well as women and minorities, face dilemmas in the face of an assumption that their public and private lives are quite separate.

How individuals actually deal with an organizational world whose rules are less and less applicable to their own situations is portrayed in many of the personal stories in this book. Two vignettes serve as an introduction; both relate to white, male business school graduates who are well established in their careers. One has changed his goals and his definitions of success in order to accommodate his private concerns better. In the other, we see no such accommodation—only the stresses (indeed, the guilt) that result.

Leo Chapman is a senior engineer with a large utility company. His wife works full-time as a contract administrator at a major university. Their two children, aged eight and ten, are involved in YMCA after-school programs and attend day camps in the summertime. Leo's day starts before his wife and children are awake: he leaves for work early so that he can pick up his children after day care in the evening. He works a forty-hour workweek—low for his organization—and devotes a great deal of time to the youth soccer program and to church activities.

In contrast, Paul Hansen is an extremely work-oriented person. After a failed entrepreneurial effort, he now works as a venture capitalist in a city two hundred miles from where his wife is employed as a banker. He has thrown himself into the new work wholeheartedly, working sixty to eighty hours per week and traveling 80 percent of the time. He rarely sees his wife and their two children. Regardless of the appearance of the situation, Paul values both his marriage and his children a great deal. He feels his relationship with his wife has facilitated his progress at work, and he appreciates the fact that she can understand his interests and concerns. Paul made arrangements to stay home for three weeks when his first daughter was born, but now seems deeply disturbed by the fact that he so rarely sees his children: "In the past year, I've been lucky to get home on weekends and am often away for six weeks at a time without seeing my kids. A new child was born six months ago, and she doesn't even recognize me." Nonetheless, he continues to work this way, and his wife remains committed to her career. A live-in au pair cares for the two babies.

The two men's aspirations are different. Leo places more value on having interesting work with competent coworkers and is not as committed to becoming financially independent. He wants regular work hours, limited travel, and what he feels is "a fair degree of responsibility," and he is satisfied in these terms. Paul also faces pressures emanating from his personal life, but he apparently feels it easier to manage the guilt he feels than to alter his commitment to work. He has no plans to change jobs in the near future.

Neither man is free of the necessity to reconcile a career with a private life. Their stories are anchored in the same dilemmas that confront their female counterparts; both men and women have to deal with the consequences of organizational demands for commitment and time. And though different people respond in different ways, the pressures exist for everyone.

PLAN OF THE BOOK

Interlude I, which follows this chapter, exemplifies the constraints within which modern couples live. It tells the story of a successful dual-career couple and the complications they face managing their lives under current conditions.

The following two chapters refine our understanding of the traditional corporate mold. Chapter 2 shows that company policies that evolved when employees could more realistically be seen as able to meet all organizational demands have resulted in a singular definition of career success and a constrained set of career paths. Such practices not only limit employees' options but also undermine the organization's needs. In Chapter 3 we see that individuals, too, reflect the traditional assumption of a separation of work and private life. Most people, when choosing occupations, do not consider how the work will impinge on their private lives. They do not understand and do not question the psychological demands of the job and how those demands can affect the kind of life they can lead—and then they are surprised by the difficulties and conflicts they encounter. These chapters are followed by Interlude II, which portrays the costs for a talented woman (and, surprisingly, for her employing organization) of following current expectations of career success.

Chapter 4 analyzes the emerging response of organizations to these issues. It shows the limitations of responses that still presume that public and private life can be dealt with as separate and gender-specific spheres. Chapters 5, 6, and 7 then identify and examine the key issues that need rethinking and on which all solutions will depend: the meaning of time, of commitment, and of career success. They outline the assumptions that need to change and provide a glimpse of new assumptions. Between Chapters 5 and 6, Interlude III portrays the cultural norms that cause the collapse of one employee's attempt to negotiate a reduced work schedule after the birth of her child—a vivid example of what needs to be rethought.

Finally, Chapter 8 presents a vision of the organizational world that would result if the traditional mold could be broken: a world in which private life is valued and legitimized, where boundaries between family and work and between male and female roles are permeable, and where organizational processes are linked to the social needs of the society.

CONCLUDING NOTE

Private life and public life can no longer be seen as conceptually separate. Too much is at stake: the equanimity of employees, the welfare of families and communities, and even the long-run viability of American companies. We need to find a way for employees to contribute to increased demands for productivity without neglecting personal needs or relying on a gendered distribution of roles.

There is no easy answer to the question of how to live in this changing world. Nor is it easy for organizations to respond to these needs, given the other pressures they currently face. The issue is clearly more complex than providing a "mommy track," even though some women may be helped by such a move. Appropriate responses to this situation go to the heart of the way that work is organized and rewarded. Change at this level is never easy; it affects the very fabric of common usage and expectation. It touches on unquestioned assumptions, and it forces one to make them explicit and to reflect on their meaning. It necessitates a new way of thinking about the link between private and public life, for both individuals and the organizations that employ them. But it is important to begin this reformulation, because what is done in this area will have a profound impact on the society in which we live and on the ability of all of us to lead productive and satisfying lives.

Interlude I

The Chases: Managing Well?

M artha and Allen Chase have two demanding careers and three small children. They are unusually successful in managing their jobs, their family, and their home, but there are special circumstances that make this success possible. A detailed description of their lives, and a full and frank commentary by Martha herself, make clear what these circumstances are and how fortunate—and unusual—is the blend of their careers.*

The Story

The Chases live in a suburb of the city in which they both work, with their three young children: a son and two daughters, one

*This case study is based on material prepared by Dr. Constance Perin for this project. It uses material from questionnaires Martha Chase reponded to five and ten years after her graduation as well as from recent interviews with her, her spouse, and their colleagues. These interviews are part of a series of networked case studies supported by the Ford Foundation under Grant 890-3012. In these case studies we started with a focal person, then interviewed the spouse, and finally moved into the employing organizations to interview peers, supervisors, and human resource persons. All the interludes are based on these case studies.

13

just recently born. Martha is a director in the financial division of a large consumer products corporation. She oversees the externally managed employee benefit funds, selecting and supervising investment management firms and insurance companies. She is also responsible for monitoring the company's managers of domestic stocks and bonds.

Allen, an economist specializing in industrial organization and econometrics, is on the antitrust staff of a large law firm specializing in mergers and takeovers. Although his job has no career track and he sees himself as atypical among social scientists, he enjoys the work. Partners rely on his expertise: he gets brought into important jobs, and a senior partner may take him to the initial meeting with board chairmen and other partners even before calling in firm associates (lawyers) on the case.

Martha received an MBA eleven years ago, at the age of twenty-four. She had just married Allen, who had been working as an economist-consultant. Three months after graduating, Martha took her first job as a financial analyst for a major multinational corporation, and Allen became a full-time graduate student in economics. Martha's job was their sole source of income; she was working between fifty to seventy hours (and spending ten hours commuting) each week. Allen was primarily responsible for shopping, cleaning, and cooking on weekdays (70 percent, compared to Martha's 30 percent).

During the first five years of her post-MBA career, Martha went through a number of phases. For the three years immediately following her degree, she felt "successful," but then there followed a period when she "became burnt out and very depressed." She had been told that she would not get ahead until she had more divisional experience, and she also felt that she had "been passed over for promotion for non-performance-related reasons." Further, she felt that her male superiors "don't feel comfortable with female professionals," and that she was "well paid [but] with little corresponding responsibilities."

But at the end of this five-year period, when Martha was promoted and "transferred from operating, financial functions to the company's investment group" her mood shifted again, as did the course of her personal and professional life. During the subsequent five years she was promoted four times and the first two of her three children (one boy, one girl) were born. Her spirits at that time were high:

> Ironically, despite becoming a working mother, I have found my niche, enjoy my job, done well, and been promoted faster than expected. In my current career/function, there are more opportunities than I originally expected five years ago. On the other hand, I am often torn between work and being a mother.

But after the birth of her third child and second daughter—a complicated pregnancy that required more leave than she had anticipated—she spoke more cautiously:

> I'm finding it tiring. Our lives are more full than after our first two children—my husband has a job and we're fixing up our house. Much depends on what I can do in the next six months. My sense is that people are sort of holding back to see what I'm able to handle, and I myself am going to have to take a month by month approach because I'm not absolutely certain of what I can handle physically and emotionally.

Nonetheless, four months later, Martha was made a director, a promotion she knew was in the works but that was delayed by her extended pregnancy leave. Asked if she was content with the new position, Martha was positive but hesitant: "Compared to everything going on with my family—in a year that I had another child—it's hard to put it into perspective. . . . I'm more concerned with the quality of my work life and home life." She has the same responsibilities as before, with the only difference now being that "I'm more visible, more under the spotlight."

Allen finished his Ph.D. one year after the couple's first child was born. At that time, they moved to the metropolitan area in which they now work and started their current jobs.

When they decided to buy a house a few years later, they also decided that Martha would continue to work, because if Martha's income were to stop, they would have needed to move to an area with lower living costs.

Now that Allen works full-time, Martha spends 25 percent more time on child care and household duties than he does. But since Allen does not have to be at his office until 9:30 or 10:00 he takes on the morning activities of feeding and dressing the children until Louise, their caretaker, arrives. Martha commutes to work via bus and cab; she arrives between 8:00 and 8:30 A.M. and tries to end her day promptly between 5:00 and 5:15 P.M. Her ability to leave the office at this time is an important element of her and Allen's complex lives. It is made possible by her seniority, rank, and the permission of her boss: "I am about the only person at my level in this office who can 'flex in' at 8:00 A.M. and 'flex out' before 5:30 P.M. on a regular basis." She thinks that the reasons why her company is "willing to put up with my personal situation" are her depth of experience and her ability to interpret key events.

> There's a lot of historical experience—how to evaluate different trends in the stock and bond markets, different investment strategies, the various investment management firms in the business today, how to interpret a day-to-day event like the big plunge in the stock market in October 1987—these sorts of things one just sort of has to know. In a way it's not enough to have somebody who's willing to work twenty-four hours a day to deal with something. There's just a lot of received wisdom, a lot of training in terms of how to handle it. It's not something that you can just pop a person into and have them work frantically for three weeks.

Martha also has a boss who sees eye to eye with her on the importance of keeping a good balance. As he describes the situation:

It all depends on your own order of priorities. I'm a believer in balance. My wife also works, and we work hard at maintaining a personal life apart from the job. We each think the other has too much dedication to our work. It's best if you stay until normal closing time and allow time for outside interests, rather than grinding away at work all the time. It's a personal choice about what you want to trade off. You have to establish priorities about what's important; the job can't take first place. In my experience, hanging around late to impress the boss just didn't do anything for me. Presence is important for when people need to see you, but not just logging in. You have to say, "This is my order of priority, and this is what's needed to get there."

Martha feels that her boss and other managers in the unit accepted her 5 o'clock limit because they were afraid of losing her. Around the time she decided to limit her day at the office, her group had been experiencing "tremendous" turnover. Investment management analysts came to her unit for "terrific exposure to the financial and investment community" and then would leave for better-paying jobs—a "revolving door" situation exacerbated by the fact that her company was behind the competition in compensation. And since it was becoming difficult for Allen to cover household tasks during the early evening hours when Martha had to work late, she took the occasion of the firm having again to hire a new person to discuss with her boss her desire for a no-matter-what quitting time.

We have come to an understanding. Sometimes I have been in the middle of pretty serious investment meetings and I would get up in front of the whole staff and I would leave between 5:00 and 5:30 P.M., and I've done that for going on three years. I think that's something I've been able to do that a lot of the men in the office haven't.

But Martha makes up for it in other ways,

> which I think I've been pretty good at, or I wouldn't have been promoted. The ways I've made up for it is that I come in very early, so I often have shown up at the office between 7:00 or 8:00 A.M. I often don't use my lunch hour. As one of my perks now, I can go to the executive dining room, but I'd rather work at my desk than go down to the dining room for about an hour talking about things of mixed value.

And since she has had a lot of experience and training, Martha understands the important investment issues, "so if a problem comes up I can troubleshoot and figure out who to call, how to solve it, get it done."

Her managerial skills have also been honed by her family experiences:

> I also think that maybe as an outgrowth of being a mother and having household responsibilities, I learned how to do things faster, organize my time for things that have to be done, to constantly reevaluate the priorities and plan ahead. And through those kinds of things, which are some of my strong points, I think that even though I walk out of the office at 5 o'clock, it isn't necessarily true that I've gotten any less work done than my colleagues, some of whom may spend more time shooting the breeze or being too long-winded in a meeting.

Asked what signals, if any, she picked up from men that they resent her leaving at 5:00 P.M., Martha pauses:

> Part of it's probably just a little bit of guilt; part of it may be internally generated or externally generated by our company's culture. But there was a time when some of my male colleagues might have seen me trundling out of the office at 5:00 P.M. carrying a briefcase, and they would say, "Short

day—you going home *already?*" Or just the looks they gave me in the elevator.

Does she think that there might also be some envy on men's part, that they cannot claim fatherhood or family obligations as a reason to leave on time?

I think that's true. Nobody has expressed it to me, partly because a lot of this is so recent. When I went on maternity leave, there had been a baby boomlet at the office, and in my absence some of these children have had their first birthdays. One of the men works long hours, and has always done that. It's part of the system, you know. He and I have had several conversations about commutes—he has a very long, three-hour daily round trip. At one time he actually commented to me about how he was going to find time to spend with his baby, and the very fact that he articulated that to me, plus the commute—clearly I'm reading things into his remarks—makes me believe that these are concerns for these men.

But for Martha it is very important to eat with her children.

I just would like to have them eat dinner with one of their parents. To have them eat dinner with *both* of their parents is really a treat. But I want to do that. I want to give them their baths, read them their story, and put them to bed. And truthfully, I'm not sure I would feel right having children and not having one of us be able to do right by them.

And so the ability to stick to a fixed stopping time is very important. But it is also complicated. It encompasses all the issues involved in the intersection of professional work and private life. And it highlights the circumstances that allow Martha to do this as well as some of the possible costs:

I began to manage my time better after the first two children, and now I try and limit what sucks up time—business lunches, nonessential business travel. In my case, I can turn down what I don't think is productive. I can control meeting times at the end of the day, for example. I don't spend enough time chatting with colleagues perhaps. I've felt that I don't have time to talk casually. I discipline myself to leave at day's end. Others don't feel they have the leeway to do this.

It also depends very much on the nature of Martha's work.

If I were in a business where I had clients and was providing a service, I wouldn't be able to say that I have to go home now and so this meeting will have to end. In law and investment banking, it's harder to claim a personal life and set limits. In some fields, even law and medicine, women can work a reduced schedule and it hurts their career. But clients also know which day they'll be in the office and can schedule their business accordingly. Doctors in group practice can fill in for each other and cover their hours. It takes the willingness of everyone to accommodate.

When Martha has a rare emergency meeting lasting beyond 5:00 P.M. or has to travel, Allen will "try to shorten his hours if he can." But it is very hard for Allen to count on ending his working day at any predictable hour, or to declare that he has to be home for dinner. So Martha sets her bounds: "There have been a couple of times that meetings have played havoc with my home life, but after making an exception a couple of times, I've let it be known that I need to leave at 5 o'clock."

Despite the stress of their complex lives, the Chases have a number of sources of support, including a neighborhood support group of ten to twenty mothers who meet monthly: "Fathers don't attend, but before and after dinner, when parents are out on the street, they talk and help each other with house repair and other chores." Martha also gets support from her mother-in-law. "Allen's mother has worked with her husband in the family business for over twenty years, and she's been very supportive of my working." Her own mother, in contrast, "was worried when I began to combine work and family life. She took a wait-and-see attitude. . . . My mother quit working forty years ago in the early years of her marriage, [though] she's been active in community relations." This legacy makes Martha, who among all her siblings has the most demanding career in addition to her very young children, wonder if it is right or wrong. "I feel I'm not following the model of being a mother. Life will not be like it was when I was growing up in the suburbs."

Martha had to take four months' leave for the birth of her third child. In her previous pregnancies, despite her company's more lenient policies, she chose to continue on the job rather than stay at home on full pay ("I worked up until about a week and a half before my due date"). And she was hoping to do something similar with this child, but then it turned out that there were complications: "I had to deal with the risk of having a premature baby, which is a serious thing. So I tried to make up for that by telecommuting." She worked at home until about four weeks before her delivery, with Louise taking the children to her house.

> I have a PC and a modem, and my colleagues found a soft-ware program that would allow me to dial up the computer at work and convert my IBM keyboard into the Digital Equipment Company keyboard we have there. I had all my files, spreadsheet programs, and access to all of our depart-ment's documents. Between that and doing an enormous amount of work by telephone, I actually got quite a bit of work done.

It took her company's voice mail system, its multiuser com-puter system, a telecommunications/software program, added telephone costs, and the support of Martha's boss to make the telecommuting possible. His attitude was critical: "We'll use it as an experiment," he told her, "to just see what we can do at home, and we'll make it a priority to get what you need to do it." But he also reported some ambivalence:

> I've spent twenty years commuting, and I realize that our functions here aren't bounded by the workplace; there's nothing really special about having to be here, except for having to meet with people now and then. Here in the office, the telephone can be your friend or your worst enemy. There are times when any of us could work at home—on a special project, for example. But my boss wants to see his people when he wants to see them, and I am not wholly comfortable with the telecommuting idea myself. I want to know that you've worked. Show me that you've got a draft or a report written.

The telecommuting experience "has been constructive," Martha declares, "because I found out how much I can get done in half an hour at home, and I intend to use that capability at work." And yet she also sees its limitations:

> I can see that the success of it obviously depends on the person instead of the work, but it also depends a lot on the child care arrangements and how old the children are. It made a big difference that my children weren't at home. My neighbor Karen stayed home for a week with a newly adopted baby, and although she had a sitter, the sitter brought a daughter along to play with Karen's older child. Those children want a lot of attention, and they drifted up to the room where Karen was trying to work. So that's an example of where children are at home, they're young, there's a new baby—telecommuting isn't going to be able to work.

Allen did not take paternity leave when his daughters were born. "There's leave available unofficially," he said, "but I didn't look into it." Asked whether men in the law firm take paternity leave, the director of professional development in Allen's firm replied, "if ten men out of this work force [of about four thousand] took time off at the birth of their child, it would be a lot. Most just go to the hospital, take a look, and come right back to work."

An interesting question is whether Allen's employer realizes that three small children create drastically different issues for his family. Martha notes that Allen's law firm and a few other firms have put together an emergency employer-sponsored day care program.

> So in that sense, the firm policy-wise has been supportive. But in terms of them saying, "Allen, you can leave this meeting," I don't know. I think there's been more sensitivity, but if they're going to be working on an important deal with a major client, they're not going to impair their ability to do the deal by letting my husband off the hook. We'll just have to deal with that.

What has helped, though, is that the pace of merger and acquisition activity has slowed down, thus lessening the pressure.

Allen is also helped by his special position in the firm. Just recently he had his first formal personnel review, and the Chases were pleased to hear that the principals "like to have him around." They were also pleased to learn that the firm does not expect him to meet the same kinds of demands on his nonprofessional time that the lawyers do. "Allen's not expected to put in long hours as a matter of form, the way they do," Martha reported, "and leaving between 6:00 and 8:00 P.M. doesn't mean a strike against him."

Besides the emergency child care network, Allen's law firm also has a part-time option, primarily for women. But part-time work means a slower career track, different kinds of work assignments, and less pay. "There are now forty-three people participating in the part-time option, of whom three are males, some of whom are involved in elder care, some pursuing other interests [such as] psychiatry, writing."

The director of professional development in Allen's firm

was asked what those who opted for part-time work could expect in terms of advancement.

> They're treated as a class. They're in their own class for salary purposes. But when they get to the point of partnership and they've been working part-time for a number of years, they're not considered for partnership. They become senior attorneys. If they elect to come back after part-time and be considered for partnership, then we'll consider where they would stand in their class—two years of full-time work needed, or what have you. So it really is an ad hoc kind of situation. We haven't had anybody come back to full-time to be considered for partner. We don't have part-time partners.

Despite such attempts by organizations to accommodate their employees' families, these issues are still very private. Martha had mentioned an assistant treasurer, a woman also on a fast track who has two children. Does Martha talk to her about their situation? Does she have a support group at work? "No, I draw support more from neighbors, relatives, and friends. I can talk frankly with them and without worrying about having the same employer." In any case, Martha notes, there are not many women with children at her company.

A number of her male colleagues have had their first children within the last eighteen months, but "the whole way that people in the workplace look at men with children is completely different, I think, from the way they look at women with children." When asked about her relationships with these colleagues, she first laughed, then hesitated and said, "In a way, it's not funny, it's sort of crazy. It's hard to discuss it with people. It's a very emotion-laden thing." Asked to be more specific about this last comment, Martha wonders whether she is projecting her own feelings on other people.

> They may not have them, and I may be totally wrong, but in other cases I believe they do have some of the same con-

cerns and feelings, based on a look, a way of saying something, casual conversations, and so on. So I sense that a lot of parents sublimate some of the stress they deal with. They either like their job and need it, or they just need to be able to perform. They're not going to go to the office and be terribly open or even allow themselves to think a lot about what's not right at the home front, either on an ongoing basis or that particular day.

There seems to be a real taboo on talking, or even thinking, about children and parenting at work. One wonders if this is a way to delegitimize the private sphere, to keep the separation of public and private in place. One wonders, too, what the emotional cost of such a taboo might be.

Comment

Are the Chases managing well? Yes, they have two successful careers and three well-cared-for children. Yet their story highlights the very special circumstances necessary to make such success possible. Martha's work can be quantified (it involves measurable deliverables) and is not subject to the demands of clients or daily crises. Her ability to control her hours—particularly her stopping time—is critical and closely connected to these characteristics of her work. Similarly, Allen is protected from some of the demands placed on lawyers on a partnership track.

It seems, then, that the particular characteristics of the Chases' work and career paths are critical. And they are fortunate also that Martha has a supportive boss and that they have found unusually good help with the children. Thus, given current organizational norms, the bounds on the possibility of combining two demanding careers with young children are rather tight. They depend on the right combination of jobs, bosses, help, and personal willingness to set priorities and limits.

CHAPTER 2

ORGANIZATIONAL CONSTRAINTS
Defining Career Success

T he Chases, portrayed in the preceding interlude, are successful in part because the work they do is not as constrained by organizational expectations about career success as
that of most employees. The lawyers in Allen's firm, the managers in Martha's company, service and sales representatives who
deal directly with customers—all of these would find it more difficult to meet their employers' expectations for top performance
if they had the same private commitments as the Chases.

And what are these expectations? What is it about organizations that makes it difficult for employees with outside responsibilities to be seen as candidates for top positions? One part of the
problem is that organizations assume that their employees are
workers only; work must come first, and all organizational de-

mands must be met. But the difficulty companies have in dealing with their employees' private lives derives also from something more general: the underlying press toward homogeneity, which obscures the differences in the goals and orientations of their workers.

Companies premise their human systems on the assumption that everyone defines success similarly and wishes to traverse one dominant career path. Incentive systems favor this modal route. Employees learn to read these monolithic signals and shape their behavior and aspirations in accordance with institutional rewards and patterns of recognition. Their personal options are constrained, as is the range of their potential contributions to their employers.

A key example of this pattern is the assumption by managers that all their employees are motivated by the desire to move up into and through the managerial hierarchy—the classic bureaucratic career.[1] Management is the ultimate goal and represents the organizational position with the highest rewards. Great emphasis is placed on management development and succession plans; employees not seen as fitting managerial criteria receive less attention, even though their contributions may be critical.

And yet we know that people enter the work force with a great variety of hopes, expectations, skills, and potentialities. They evolve a variety of career orientations, only some of which fit the linear patterns of movement up a managerial hierarchy. This disjunction between the needs and satisfactions of employees and the inflexible assumptions on which the career paths available to them are based is a critical organizational constraint on the ability of workers to contribute fully to their companies without jeopardizing their personal needs.[2]

Though pressures for uniformity in career procedures stem in part from current demands for equality of opportunity, they have long existed for other reasons. They derive ultimately from the attitudes of the managers who determine the shape of career systems. These managers, themselves a relatively homogeneous group, assume that the story of their career success defines the contours and the necessary characteristics of all successful careers. And so they opt for "homosocial reproduction," recruiting employees who fit the mold of those already in the organization.[3] Such cloning may increase the level of comfort of managers, but it acts as a deep-seated barrier to adjusting organizational practice to the complex realities of a diverse work force. It reflects expectations that are constraining and counterproductive, and it creates a disabling contradiction between work and career.

To understand this contradiction in any detail, one must distinguish between employees who are chiefly involved with the actual work of their occupational role and those who are concerned more with their status within an organizational setting. Allen and Martha Chase, for example, clearly enjoy the work they do and perform very well. They contribute to their employing organizations in very special ways, having found positions that fit both their particular talents and their private needs. The problem is that traditional organizational practice makes such mutually beneficial accommodations difficult.

Take, for example, the case of Christopher Bates. Trained as an engineer, Chris describes the personal gratification he gets from working as follows: "One of the advantages in engineering is that you can see the product of your efforts, something tangible that you are responsible for, some concrete contribution that can make you feel proud of yourself." For him the work feeds directly into his feelings of self-worth: "In some professions you never know whether you succeed or fail. You can convince yourself, but you never have solid proof whether you have done well. That's the advantage of hard-core engineering. You know you can't fool yourself very long." Yet, ironically and significantly, Chris said that he feels no particular commitment to his work and thinks he should have gone into a different field altogether.[4]

This complex response reflects a basic dilemma: success is defined externally as hierarchical advancement, but often the work that is most personally satisfying—and most critical to organizational performance—lies elsewhere. Some of the negative consequences of this situation are apparent in the following description of a supervisor who was seen to be ineffective as a manager:

He was promoted because he is technically terrific. He was pushed into supervision. He could have refused, but everybody accepts because of salary and prestige. But he finds it hard to let go of the day-to-day tasks . . . It is not intentional, but he is so involved. He loves the work so much that he can't stop himself.

Another example of the constraining effect of this emphasis on position and advancement comes from a comparison of home-based computer specialists with an equivalent group in an office-based setting. To the home-based group, the meaning of the occupational role centered on an intrinsic involvement with the actual tasks they were performing. Their concerns centered on having interesting work, the significance of their tasks, and keeping up their skills. They showed relatively little concern for success defined in the traditional way. The office-based group, in contrast, exhibited a high degree of involvement in their careers as such. Caught in the traditional emphasis on career advancement, they were concerned more with status, prestige, and success as defined by promotions and pay, and less with the tasks, or with keeping up skills.[5]

The organizationally and socially accepted definition of career success inculcates an orientation toward career advancement at the expense of the work itself. And yet such an orientation can interfere decisively with organizational effectiveness. In many companies, advancement necessitates visibility to management, but effective work demands involvement and responsibility at the nonsupervisory level. For example, assume that a customer with a complaint about a system approaches the system's designer, who recognizes the problem as one of development. At this point two scenarios are possible, one emphasizing the needs of work, the other the needs of career. The work scenario has the designer and the developer sitting down together with the customer to diagnose the problem. After some deliberation, the issue is resolved, the customer is pleased, and the developer is not embarrassed. But in the career scenario, the designer seeks credit from management for this effort by turning to his or her manager, who then contacts the developer's manager, who in turn deals with the developer. Since the process takes longer, the customer is less satisfied and the relationship between developer and designer becomes strained, making future coordination between them more difficult. The work suffers, but the career of the designer is advanced within the monolithic, hierarchical career structure.[6]

As companies try to become more responsive to customer needs, their hope is to eliminate such maneuvering. But they will not succeed as long as hierarchical advancement remains the operative definition of career success, buttressed by human resource practices that depend on individualistic indicators of what is considered good performance. It is no accident, for example, that Deming—the father of the quality movement—believes that if businesses are going to be successful in global competition, they must "remove barriers that rob people in management and in engineering of their right to pride of workmanship, [which means] abolishment of the annual [performance] or merit rating and of management by objectives."[7]

Thus traditional assumptions about careers and career success, along with the human resource practices that reinforce them, are barriers both to organizational competitiveness and to the ability of employees to respond to their private concerns. Neither the home-based computer specialists nor the Chases—both of whom found ways of integrating work with the needs of their private lives—were caught by the traditional definition of what it means to have a successful career. Unfortunately, however, their circumstances remain unusual.

Even the one consistent attempt by some companies to recognize a dual ladder in careers has had its difficulties.[8] These companies, following the model of the aerospace industry, have instituted professional ladders designed for employees who wish to stay intimately involved with the work for which they were trained. By defining this alternate route as a ladder, however, they nonetheless assume that advancement issues are paramount. Emphasis is placed on providing a hierarchical structure in the alternate route that parallels that of the managerial career. Even in these companies, therefore, one sees evidence of the traditional belief in uniformity of aspirations.

Sales is perhaps one organizational role that does not fit into this pattern.[9] Salespeople often decline promotions to management in order to retain the freedom from organizational demands they enjoy in their positions, and compensation schemes for sales positions may even allow the most successful to outearn their managers. But sales is a highly individualistic function; it may attract only certain kinds of people, and reward and recognition systems that work there may be more difficult to apply to more interdependent organizational roles.

The emphasis on uniformity also makes it difficult for companies to acknowledge employees' personal needs. Even before family issues were explicitly acknowledged as relevant to career patterns, there was evidence of a complicated pull between work and private concerns. In 1970, for example, fully one-third of midcareer workers with engineering degrees—all men—who were good performers in their jobs were nonetheless almost exclusively oriented to their families, their communities, or their nonvocational interests.[10] And Schein, in his original classification of the career anchors of male managers, found that some were anchored to a particular geographical location, not to any aspect of their work or career.[11] Significantly, these studies also showed that employers had no idea how to deal with these people.

Nor are career orientations necessarily constant over a lifetime. In one nine-year period, for example, it was found that men who stayed in their functional specialties became more involved with their families and other private concerns; those who had been moved to managerial positions became more involved with their organizational roles.[12] And Evans and Bartolome, in their study of successful male European managers, showed that the first career decade was highly organizationally oriented, but during the second decade managers were more likely to turn their attention to their families. Only in a third decade, with career and family both well established and the immediate demands from both somewhat lessened, did these managers find it possible to integrate the two domains.[13]

Thus issues of family have always been intertwined with occupational experiences, and the presumed contradiction between an underlying orientation to one's public or private world is even more of an issue today than it was at the time of the studies from which the examples above are taken. The classic distinction between people who work to live and those who live to work is anchored in a notion of individual choice. But we now know that such choice is heavily constrained by relatively unquestioned organizational procedures. Both social and economic change have transformed this "choice" into a dilemma that confronts employees at all points on the occupational scale and at various periods in their lives.

MULTIPLE CAREER PATHS[14]

We have already mentioned managerial and professional career paths, as evidenced in the so-called dual ladder. Though both are based on the assumption of the importance of hierarchical advancement, they at least are visible reminders that people's orientations differ. But they do not cover all interests, even of seemingly homogeneous groups. There also are orientations based not on hierarchical advancement but on movement from one interesting assignment to another or on coordinating roles (for example, transferring with technology one has helped develop into the division or field where it is used). These nonhierarchical movements are rarely explicitly acknowledged, and hence the mechanisms that would make them both productive and satisfying rarely exist. Any of these orientations, moreover, could be associated with major involvement with private concerns, as long as this is deemed legitimate and human resource practices are adjusted accordingly.

The managerial route, as already indicated, is deemed most "successful" and the one most in need of sole involvement with and commitment to work. In most organizations it is the most explicitly detailed, the most obvious, and for many the most attractive. It carries with it the highest compensation and prestige, explained by one R & D employee as follows: "Managers move much more quickly and have better working conditions—[they] get cars, secretaries, a dining room, and phones. They have carpets and curtains." But despite these attractions there are also some misgivings, as is evident in the comments of a number of independent contributors:

> The managerial obviously dominates. I have mixed emotions personally whether I would enjoy it. It is tempting because of the money, but for the job satisfaction I am not convinced that it would be pleasant.

> Management I would like. Everyone wants it. But when one looks at management I wonder why. What seems to happen is that at every level the only thing you want is the next level.

Part of the problem stems from the fact that managers are assumed to be the most competent and are given the authority to make decisions. This assumption is often contradicted, however, by the reality of the manager's actual situation. As managers move up they gain responsibility for a greater variety of functions and projects, and thus they are less likely to be expert in all the processes involved in the work for which they are responsible. Also, to be successful they must necessarily develop skills in new tasks—particularly budgeting, the evaluation of people, and liaison activities with other organizational units.

This combination of being assumed to be the most competent while being responsible for more tasks lies behind the pressures of this path.[15] It leads managers to feel they must be available at all times to their employees, and it makes it more difficult for them to delegate responsibility to other people or to empower their staff. One manager in an administrative unit of a manufacturing company, for example, felt that if her employees took advantage of the corporate policy on flextime, her day would have to be extended by two hours at either end in order to "cover" her people. Not only was the effect of this presumption a burden for her, but it discouraged her subordinates from taking advantage of the flexibility offered and unnecessarily reinforced their sense of dependence on the manager to accomplish their tasks.

A contrasting example comes from an innovative arrangement that evolved in the central R & D lab of one large electronics company.[16] In that case, the person promoted to management was *not* the best technically but the one most willing and able to do the administrative tasks required. The promotion thus was more an assignment to a new set of tasks than a reward for technical excellence. The group's technical superstar served as an informal co-leader, and it was he who made the technical decisions for the group (though they were announced as joint decisions). He then pursued his scientific work, only participating in formal group activities when there were technical presentations for potential backers of the research. The manager took care of all the administrative tasks, managed the evaluation and development of the people in the group, and worried about getting the resources needed. It was a successful arrangement that worked because the manager, who gave up pretension of technical dominance, was proud of the expertise and competence of his "subordinate" and openly depended on him for technical advice. And the scientist, who had no ambitions for a title, was financially rewarded in line with his actual level of authority, not his formal hierarchical position.

It is interesting to note that this group was in a division led by a female manager, a highly respected physicist whose explicit philosophy was to work through her people and not get involved herself in the technical work. Such an empowering philosophy is necessary for an arrangement like this to work in the traditional bureaucratic setting, and it requires also mutual respect and trust among the people involved. In the end, though, it depends on legitimizing and formally recognizing a variety of orientations, and on personnel procedures that allow organizations to reward people in line with their performance at the tasks in which they are engaged, rather than the formal position they occupy.

Many companies have come to recognize some of the negative consequences of overemphasis on the managerial route to success, and frequently they have tried to define an alternative career path in which "advancement" is possible without shifting to management. But as already indicated, it does not often work, since the traditional culture still values these paths differentially. As one employee reported, "There is supposed to be a professional ladder here, but I do not see it in effect. They are not as high as managers." Only under special conditions was it seen as possibly beneficial ("The professional path would be best for a female doing the kind of work that I am, because there is less opportunity for discrimination").

The problem is that movement along this path often does not lead to an increase in authority or organizational influence. It has been described as a rungless ladder: there are no rungs because nothing changes in one's work or organizational functioning as one moves up this ladder. Nor does such "advancement" necessarily increase one's visibility or status, since the main difference it makes is to increase one's salary, a reward that is private and thus precludes the public recognition accompanying a managerial promotion. And even title changes or visible changes in perks are ephemeral forms of recognition if no added responsibility or authority accompanies the move.

In response to these difficulties, some companies have tried to build into the system a reward process based on peer reviews from inside and outside the company. But in industry, those people whose work is most likely to be rewarded by such criteria are probably the least in need of organizational recognition, since they are likely to be more oriented to the external professional world.[17] Further, the introduction of an academic-like judgment creates an even steeper pyramid than exists on the management side, since it relegates a large proportion to inferior statuses. In one company that prides itself on its recognition of professional excellence, for example, 83 percent of those on the professional ladder are at the first point of the progression, as compared to only 42 percent of those on the managerial side.[18] Indeed, many companies have positions high on their professional ladders with no people in them at all. This situation leads to comments like the following:

> They say we have a dual ladder, and maybe we have it, but it is more lip service; there are very few people on it.

> In the professional path I am a strong believer. It does exist, but not enough. It has done well for me and a few others, but realistically it is pretty flimsy—very narrow.

It is very difficult to deal with these structural constraints on the professional ladder. In situations where the career path is not artificially constrained, it serves as a convenient dumping ground for plateaued managers and becomes seen as clearly second-rate. In those cases where it is supposedly working well, the constraints imposed limit its benefits to those few highly educated employees who are primarily rewarded and motivated by their reputation in the global professional community. What is really involved, and seldom recognized, is the questionable assumption on which the concept of the dual ladder is based: that organizational success equals hierarchical advancement.

We know that there are employees with different concerns; as already mentioned, some desire only to have a series of interesting and challenging assignments on which to work.[19] One would think that it would be relatively easy to ensure a series of challenging assignments and to specify the procedures to support such a career route.[20] The problem is that there is a tendency in most companies to push employees in the direction of narrow specialization:

> Initially there were varied projects, but then you get funneled in. You work for recognition, and you become the focal point and work only in that area.

In bureaucratic settings, where the "logic of advancement" holds,[21] employees with this orientation—who may in the end be the ones most responsible for the company's productivity—tend not to receive much attention.

The people who would like to follow such a career path get pigeonholed into repetitive assignments with little organizational recognition. They are then likely to become dissastisfied and to show the characteristic drop in performance associated with older employees. These consequences, however, are more a reflection of a poorly managed career path than of any inevitable decline with age. This group is most subject to salary compression: younger people come in with higher and higher starting salaries, and rates of increase tend to decrease with age. Combined with the push toward narrow specialization, these factors actually contribute to the decline they seemingly only reflect.[22]

A useful, truly creative pattern of movement among challenging assignments could combine productive work with personal concerns. Flexibility could be introduced between assignments, and time and location could more easily be controlled.

In one company, for example, the computer regularly identified those employees who had been in their current assignments for more than four years, and personal attention was then given to their development. In another case, management insisted (by monitoring and evaluation) that 10 percent of each employee's time be spent learning a new technology, which then would lead to a new assignment. Discretionary time for personal concerns and sabbatical leaves have also occasionally been seen as useful for this group.[23] In all cases, reward systems have to be devised that assume and help create continued high performance. As clearly stated by one industrial scientist, employees do adjust to what they perceive is expected of them: "The flattening of the salary curve assumes that older professionals are less productive. And since salary is the dominant mechanism, they are forced into being less productive."

One form of new challenge, without hierarchical advancement, would be to cross functional boundaries.[24] Such movement could provide a valued change in the conditions of work, and it could also help the coordination needs of the company. But despite these obvious advantages, it is usually not part of any systematically defined career path.[25] And there are structural barriers that make crossing boundaries difficult in many companies, particularly when human resource procedures are rigidly defined and uniformly applied. R & D employees, for example, may have salaries that are only matched by employees in other parts of the company who have large management responsibility. Such a situation was described by professionals in one R & D lab:

> This is a problem. I am told that it is a salary problem, that at the research lab we are so highly paid that to get to the same salary in the operating divisions you would have to have one hundred people working for you.

> In my level in a division you would have to have fifty people to get the same pay. That is a barrier to transfer.

Removing such structural constraints, however, would make it possible to achieve the organizational and personal advantages of this path. One forty-seven-year-old engineer in an electronics design unit, for example, wanted to move to another location for personal reasons. He negotiated with his supervisor to shift from being a design engineer to being a product engineer so that he could develop the skills he would need to be transferred to a production facility opening up in the area where he wanted to live. And though he used to get "real satisfaction" from designing—"an interesting job because you work from beginning to end, and you see everything"—he saw the production work as an "interesting new challenge." The transfer to the production unit he wanted took place, and he did not leave the company. He is now personally more satisfied and, because of his design experience, is also particularly useful to his employer in the new job.

CONCLUDING NOTE

Clearly, individual orientations and organizational career paths often are not congruent, and this fact has negative consequences for both employee satisfaction and organizational effectiveness. In particular, organizational procedures are likely to be based on the assumptions that high-level employees are totally involved in the public, occupational part of their lives and are concerned primarily with moving up a managerial hierarchy. Standard career mechanisms tend to reinforce (or inculcate) an orientation to career advancement rather than to the work itself. And this continues to happen at a time when demographic change is bringing employees' private, family concerns into bold relief, and when organizations are moving toward fewer hierarchical levels and greater emphasis on the task responsibility of all their employees.

CHAPTER 3

INDIVIDUAL CONSTRAINTS

Occupational Demands and Private Life

O rganizations make it difficult to maintain meaningful links between public and private life in part because the career paths they provide and their definitions of career success presume a natural, normal separation of the two spheres. In thinking about their occupations individuals also assume an inevitable separation of work and private life. We saw a subtle illustration of this in the story of the Chases, who (though remarkably successful in their life arrangements) felt it inappropriate to talk at work about their children and the management of their care.

Similarly, when individuals consider occupational choice, the typical emphasis is on the skills that a particular occupation requires and the material benefits that it can provide. Often ignored are other aspects of a job—what might be called its psychological demands—that profoundly affect the type of life one can lead. The goal of this chapter is to identify these important occupational characteristics so that their impact can be anticipated.

One set of concerns stems from the conditions surrounding the work. What is the level of absorption that the job requires? How much of one's total time must be devoted to it? Is one able to choose where to work and where to live? These conditions, which affect employees' time, their cognitive and emotional involvements, and the extent to which they are subject to organizational control, are what Kanter has referred to as the *absorptiveness* of an occupational role.[1]

But there is also another, less obvious consideration: the overlap between the attitudes and skills required by the work and those needed to deal successfully with family and community concerns. Some occupational roles emphasize attributes highly relevant to successful relations in one's private life—for example, interpersonal skills, the ability to communicate, and self-insight. Other work depends on skills that do not have this overlap—the work of a mathematician, for instance.[2]

Finally, is there a difference between the reactions of an employee whose private responsibilities are taken care of by a spouse—the model on which most organizational practice is based—and those of the growing number of people for whom this traditional pattern no longer exists? To answer this question, one must consider specifically how an occupational role affects workers without traditional family support systems, who are faced with the necessity of integrating family and work in innovative ways. Primarily this refers to women, but it applies also to men in single-parent or dual-career families, who also face family pressures that are different from those of their more traditional peers. All existing evidence indicates that the number of these "nontraditional" workers is increasing. Hence the special challenges they face from the psychological demands of work are of critical importance not only to them but also to the organizations that depend on their contributions.

Thus, to explore the way occupations affect the integration of one's life, three questions are relevant. First, what skills and attitudes are required by the work, and how do they relate to good family and community relations—is there any overlap or complementarity between the activities of the occupational and the personal role? Second, how constraining on a person's personal life are the organizationally imposed conditions for career success? This second question concerns the personal consequences of the organizational definition of success discussed in the previous chapter in terms of its organizational implications. And third, is there something special about the way women, and men without traditional family support, react to these psychological demands? Occupational differences on these questions can have a significant impact on people's ability to be both professionally and privately successful and satisfied.

To gain greater clarity and more detail in understanding the implications of such differences, I turn in this chapter to the specific psychological demands associated with three types of occupational roles. Two of these are prototypes of corporate roles: the managerial role and the independent contributor role. The third—the academic role—is useful because it represents an occupational position with seemingly great autonomy and discretion over the conditions of work, which should make it easier to link occupational and private life. The reality is more complicated, however, since the flexibility possible in this role is accompanied by internalized pressures that can negate its benefits. An analysis of the demands on professors' private lives therefore is an important backdrop to any attempt to improve the lives of people who work in the corporate world.

These three types of occupational roles all involve different challenges to employees' private lives and different relationships between the private and public worlds. All three are potentially satisfying occupations, and all could be filled by the same people; an engineering graduate, for example, might end up in any of these positions. Yet each role presents its occupants with very different psychological requirements and very different opportunities for particular life-styles.

MANAGERS

Managers are accountable for results over which they have no direct control, results that depend on the work done by the people they supervise.[3] The skills required of them—which are more interpersonal than technical—are similar to those necessary to make private relationships satisfactory, and they should ease the link between public and private life. Also, management is an occupation in which incoming information can be processed quickly, and need not be mentally stored for long periods of time before it can be transformed into usable output.[4] Close observation of managers has shown that their daily tasks are often a series of quick, fragmented communications: over the phone, in meetings, with people met in passing.[5] It is a job with a great variety of situationally triggered actions. It is highly pressured but, because of its more fragmented nature, is not likely to be subject to mental overload, which should make it easier to attend to private needs. In fact, a common procedure for assessing management potential is the in-basket exercise, in which a person is required to deal with many disparate requests and bits of information in a very short period of time. People who put these items into a pile to be dealt with later—a frequent academic response—are not likely to be judged as good management material.

The best managers also learn in making decisions to depend as much on the ideas and views of peers, subordinates, and consultants as they do on their own. Hence sharing of information and receiving as well as giving advice (again, characteristics important in private life) are critical parts of the manager's job. In this respect the managerial role is quite different from the doctor or lawyer, whose professional identity is based on the personal mastery of highly specialized knowledge of which he or she alone is the expert. But though the actual activities required of managers seem highly complementary to the skills required of good personal and family relations off the job, the conditions of the work—the demands imposed by the organizational definition of career success—create pressures in a contrary direction.

Managers often enter organizations as independent contributors, but are soon identified as having management potential. The initial career years are critical, for the probability of moving up a management track decreases dramatically if there is no initial promotion to a supervisory position during these years.[6] Hence a prerequisite for future success is primary commitment to work and career, which creates obvious difficulties in a period of life that is usually associated with starting a family of one's own.

There are also no clear, unambiguous criteria of performance; it is hard to judge an individual manager's work. But judgments have to be made, and so great emphasis tends to be placed on substitute indicators, such as time put in and evidence of ambition. The fact that managers are expected to go where the organization sends them, to pursue the tasks that it defines, and to subordinate their private needs in numerous ways to those of their employers imposes real constraints on the ability of managers to mesh the demands of work with those of private life. Thus the complementarity between characteristics deemed necessary for managerial activities and for nonwork concerns, which should ease the integration of work and family, is offset by the organization's demand for a manager's complete and exclusive loyalty.

The nature of its activities should make management a good career for women, since it requires interdependence and such "feminine" skills as tolerance in dealing with people and with ambiguity. Indeed, explicit calls have appeared for managers with characteristics more akin to what have come to be seen as feminine traits.[7] This nontraditional part of the work force ought to find an even greater complementarity between managerial activities and personal life. But this presumption ignores the stereotyped and gendered expectations of what constitutes power and authority, which women have more difficulty in meeting.

Nor is it easy for women, or for single-parent and dual-career men, to combine a managerial role with a family, since the organization's demands almost require traditional family support. It therefore is not surprising that research shows most successful managers are married men with traditional families. Women managers are much more likely to be single and, if married, are less likely to have children.

The demands for relocation are another example. Employees (whether male or female) whose spouses also have careers face issues surrounding the dual career; those who are single face isolation. The man with traditional family support faces neither. And even though companies such as IBM and General Motors are introducing guidelines on how to deal with dual-career couples in relocation decisions, they are not generally questioning the assumption that frequent geographical movement is necessary for the development of their managers. Further, though companies have made some progress in addressing the movement of dual-career couples when both of them work for the same company, the problems people face when they work in different organizations, or have different careers altogether, are more difficult.[8]

Finally, the use of "face time" (being visibly seen to be at work and always available when needed) as an indicator of successful performance puts anyone with serious commitments in the private sphere at a disadvantage. As is discussed elsewhere in this book, such a criterion may induce behavior that responds less to the actual needs of the work than to stereotyped, habitual organizational expectations. In many ways, therefore, the managerial career as currently defined presents more difficulties to nontraditional employees than it does to those who have traditional family support. And it is particularly difficult for women, despite the ironic situation that it emphasizes skills presumably more characteristic of the female part of the population.

Data from a follow-up of MBA recipients five and ten years after acquiring their degrees confirm the differential impact of these "requirements" on men and women. After five years, women with MBAs had reached the same hierarchical levels (with more or less equal salaries) as their male peers, but they had done so with greater stress and by working longer hours.[9] Presumably they felt this to be necessary in order to establish their credibility in an occupation in which there were few women who had proven their ability to move to the top. But the situation did not remain this way; on the contrary, over the next five years men's stress greatly increased, whereas that of women decreased.

Thus, ten years after receiving their MBAs, the women managed to find ways to cope with stress in both their work and personal lives. Some changed their aspirations and either entered a different field or career or left business altogether. Others found accommodations within the career itself, by changing their employment conditions with regard to the amount or location of work or, in some cases, by becoming self-employed. In general, these changes led to greater job satisfaction (and a great sense of security) and, interestingly, caused women to feel more successful. But the criteria they used to judge their success were different from those of the men: both work considerations and personal satisfactions were relevant, and a sizable group specifically mentioned balance as a key ingredient to their feelings of success.

But what was successful for these individual women may not have been seen as successful for the companies that employed them, since many gained their greater equilibrium by leaving the fast-track corporate careers on which they had embarked. If companies are seriously interested in advancing women into top management, they need to think about the requirements these careers impose on their employees.

Ten years after receiving their MBAs, the men had a very different reaction than their female counterparts. They said that they tended to ignore stress altogether or simply to "try harder," and a few reported that they coped by *increasing* the segmentation between their work and their personal lives—a response not given by any woman in the sample. In judging their success, most of the men used only work criteria; their personal lives appeared to be seen as entirely separate. The men found it difficult to bring their work and family lives together, and their tendency was to keep the two spheres as separate as possible. The women tended to see a positive interrelation among their work, their partner's work, and their personal relationship, but the men either saw no effect of one on the other or tended to feel that the relationship caused problems.[10]

What these findings seem to indicate is that more women than men have found ways to reduce stress, and that they have done so by bridging the public and private domains. But though they have gained personal satisfaction from the arrangements they have forged, their ambitions have had to be curtailed. In a number of cases, for example, valued female employees negotiated for less time in the office after returning from maternity leave, though they realized that such an arrangement was likely to have a permanent effect on the course of their careers. The flexibility they needed—while enhancing their lives, reducing stress, and responding to family needs—went against expected managerial behavior in their employing organizations.

The excessive time demands of management, which make private concerns so problematic, are assumed to reflect the requirements of work. It seems equally plausible, though, that these demands are constructed as a way of measuring individual worth in situations where performance criteria are difficult or impossible to specify. The detailed interviews conducted by myself and my colleagues indicate the importance of being visible, to be *seen* as giving one's all to work, in order to have one's performance judged positively. Only then is flexibility granted as a special privilege.[11] And as the experience of women seems to indicate, even when flexibility is granted, there may still be negative career consequences.

INDEPENDENT CONTRIBUTORS

In contrast to managers, independent contributors are directly responsible for the work they do. Most have specialist training (financial, technical, legal, personnel, and so forth). On the whole, therefore, their main activities have no immediate complementarity with those required for personal relationships.[12] Such lack of complementarity might be expected to make it more difficult for most independent contributors to integrate their occupational and private lives; for example, many engineers report that they are more at ease with things than with people.[13] But perhaps unexpectedly, these conditions of work seem not to create difficulties in linking occupational life with private concerns.

As already indicated, the organizational definition of hierarchical advancement as the primary success route leaves many independent contributors in jobs that no longer energize them—and therefore they channel their energies into activities closer to home. Most still perform well and continue to be satisfied with their jobs and with their careers, but their commitments shift to a more balanced state.

The independent contributor role, therefore, seems to make it easier to live an integrated life. But is this also true for those who do not fit the traditional mold? Women in these roles—particularly in the more technical ones—confront problems that stem from gendered stereotypes of the requirements of the work. For them, the lack of complementarity of the skills needed for the job may make the link between their work and private lives more complicated.

Consider the findings of a study comparing male and female engineers. Even though the two groups were equal in most aspects of their careers (positions, actual work, salaries, and even orientations to work) their technical competence was experienced differently. For the men, an emphasis on technical competence went along with perceived success and self-confidence. But for the women, self-confidence was actually lower when they ascribed greater importance to their technical competence. Therefore, the relation between their work and personal lives outside of work was complicated by the character of the work they did.[14]

This difference reflects once again the difficulty experienced by people who do not fit homogeneous organizational expectations. Since technical work has been largely a role for men, expectations surrounding it are likely to fit more easily into their life experiences. It is intriguing to note, though, that men whose wives were also engineers or scientists showed the same ambivalence about technical expertise as the women. These men, like their female counterparts, are nontraditional; they share to an unusual degree both professional and family concerns with their wives. But because they function in an occupational role that is premised on the assumption that work is entirely separable from one's private life, they find the role more complicated.

It therefore seems that the independent contributor role does allow some people to live satisfactory work and private lives. But for women, as well as for men married to equally trained and career-oriented wives, there is evidence that the way the career has been conceived can create significant complications.

PROFESSORS

In contradistinction to these corporate careers, what can be said about the effect of a professorial role on one's private life? Generally the psychological demands on professors are embedded in the distinctive characteristics of academic life. First, the university setting differs from that of industry in that the expectation of a lifelong technical career is fulfillable (even expected), and a managerial role is not considered to be the most successful career path (often, in fact, the least successful). Second, universities have rigid timetables. The seven-year up-or-out tenure rule sharply divides one's career into two segments: the years before tenure, with one clearly specified goal (publish or perish), and the much longer period after tenure, in which standards and guidelines are assumed to be internalized. In the latter period the academic career has fewer milestones and fewer checkpoints than most other professional career paths. It also has fewer clearly specified requirements; often the only time one's presence is essential is during classes, which typically do not occupy much more than six hours a week. In addition, one has a long summer vacation.

These characteristics seem to make the academic career ideal for individual satisfaction and for linking one's employment to the needs of one's private life. Unfortunately the evidence proves the opposite, which is why an analysis of this career is critical as one considers changing the shape of work in the corporate world.

The lack of external requirements or specific career goals actually makes the internal pressures of the academic role greater. Comparisons tend to be made with those few signs of achievement that do exist in the system: named university chairs, Nobel Prizes, and the like. Since these affect only the exceptional few, the great majority are doomed, to some degree, to feelings of inadequacy and a lack of appreciation.[15] It is the very lack of formal signals of achievement that contributes to the frenetic quality of academic life.

People in academic careers also face a multiplicity of demands. Rewards tend to come from scholarly research, an activity that creates a great deal of mental overload. Research is a long-range activity and needs constant attention; successful books cannot be written in small fragments. Thus, in an academic career, there is much input but relatively little and long-delayed output. On top of this, professors must prepare and teach their classes, serve on administrative committees, and interact with outside professional, governmental, and industrial organizations. The combination of a multiplicity of demands and the mental overload from the activities that produce new knowledge profoundly affects the ability of professors to combine work with satisfactory and meaningful personal lives.

Neither the character of the activities involved in being a professor nor the conditions surrounding the career make a balance between work and private life easily attainable. In fact, professors have an unusually difficult time integrating work and family. Despite the seeming flexibility of their working lives, their occupations are highly absorptive, primarily because they have internalized a complex set of demands. Moreover, their work activities offer little help. Academic occupational norms (like those of doctors and lawyers) assume that each incumbent is an expert in his or her own right. Both as scholars and as teachers, professors present themselves as sources of truth and knowledge and models for what is deemed appropriate and right.

These problems are exacerbated by the fact that professors, more than managers or independent contributors, are likely to have spouses who themselves are professionals, and hence they are subject to the compelling demands for commitment to the private sphere characteristic of dual-career families. Given the structure of academic careers, these conflicting demands are more likely to lead to strain than to any accommodation to one's family. For example, professors far along in their careers tend to be *less* accommodative to family and *more* involved with career success than are their junior colleagues—the exact opposite of the pattern for independent contributors.[16]

The academic career therefore is paradoxical. Despite its advantages of independence and flexibility, it is psychologically difficult. The lack of ability to limit work, the tendency to compare oneself primarily to the exceptional giants in one's field, and the high incidence of overload make it particularly difficult for academics to find a satisfactory integration of work with private life. It is important to remember these difficulties as we consider shifting corporate careers from structured moves up hierarchical ladders to livelihoods built on normative involvement with loosely defined missions and goals.

Moreover, though the demand of the academic life for full emotional and cognitive involvement—its absorptiveness—affects all people in it, it seems to be a particular strain for women, especially if there are children involved. Data from a survey of professors at a large technical university show that the median workload is almost sixty hours per week, and more than 10 percent spend upward of seventy-five hours on their professional work.[17] And even though most faculty members acknowledge a fair degree of control over the scheduling of their work hours, the total amount of time seen as necessary for promotion, tenure, and distinctive accomplishment supersedes the advantages of control. This personal dilemma is vividly described by one university professor:

> I cannot ask for more flexibility; it is the total amount of work that does me in. I love my family and value the time I

51

spend with them. I also love my work and the time I spend in the lab. It is the great conflict of my life. I have not achieved a satisfactory solution. Most of the anger that I ever carry is due to this friction.

Women without children report even longer hours than their male colleagues, the result of greater difficulty in establishing their credibility. With children, however, the women's (but not the men's) hours drop significantly, and their career chances become jeopardized under current rules.

It is the unbounded nature of the academic career that is the heart of the problem. Time is critical for professors, because there is not enough of it to do all the things their job requires: teaching, research, and institutional and professional service. It is therefore impossible for faculty members to protect other aspects of their lives, and work tends to dominate. These comments by two senior male professors are by no means unique:

> The existing pattern of time demands on a faculty member degrades the quality of life to an unacceptable degree in my case. The problem is not time pressure per se; rather it is the number of separate factors that are able to make independent and uncontrollable demands on my time. . . . I am not living with a partner largely because I cannot command the hours/week that any reasonable relationship demands. . . . Early retirement is a serious option if I cannot effect a substantial improvement in my situation.

> Since marriage in 1954, my time has been essentially devoted to my profession (student to professor), e.g., 7 days/week throughout the year. My wife was responsible for raising four children and now cares for our grandchildren. About five years ago we did start to have a family vacation. I would like to live a more normal life, but pressure keeps increasing to increase my productivity. I am looking forward to partial retirement ASAP (say, a 40–50-hour week).

The data from the survey that elicited these remarks showed that women faculty in the university were much less likely to have children, or to expect ever to have children, than was the case for their male colleagues. But close analysis reveals that it is not sex but dual-career status that mainly accounts for this difference. The major distinction proves to be not that between men and women but between men whose wives provide family support for them and those professors (both male and female) whose partners are equally involved in demanding careers; the former are much more likely to have children than the latter. A normal family life seems difficult for any professor who lacks a spouse to take care of the home. Everyone, it seems, needs a "wife."

We must therefore be careful that we do not change corporate careers by increasing apparent flexibility while at the same time increasing the unboundedness of expectations. And we must watch that we do not impose on women the additional demands that are often evident in university life. Faculty women are frequently asked to carry—or perhaps they set for themselves—a very heavy agenda of involvements with committees, students, and women's affairs. They are on call from administrations seeking to ensure the participation of women in decision making, but since there are relatively few of them, their load is heavier than that of their male colleagues. Also, students may find it easier to "burden" female teachers with their concerns. Though time-consuming, some of these roles take place behind the scenes, and the women involved may get no official credit.[18] This enhances the tendency of women to be invisible, to be valued less than their male colleagues. Though seemingly contradictory, both extremes of women's roles—their overinvolvement and their invisibility—make it more difficult for them to meet the traditional requirements for promotion and tenure.

The situation is both helped and complicated by affirmative action efforts, which have greatly increased the number of women in academia, particularly at the lower ranks, and have eased their situation considerably. But there are also possible psychological costs. The general difficulties academic careers present to a person's self-esteem are exacerbated in situations where an individual, or her colleagues, might think that without affirmative action she would not be there at all. These tendencies are also evident in the corporate setting. They add a special occupational burden to women who already carry most of the responsibility for linking public and private life.

CONCLUDING NOTE

Thus each of these occupational roles—despite similarities in the extent of initial training required and in the standard of living provided—entails different psychological demands and different satisfactions and rewards, which have profound effects on the private lives of those involved. For managers, there seems to be a complementarity between the activities and skills needed on the job and those required off it. But the organizational demands require that the family be subservient to the primary career, particularly during the early years. In contrast, for many independent contributors (whose spheres of activities are not in themselves complementary), the organizational tendency to decrease the challenge of the job is likely to create the opportunity for an easier integration between work and nonwork. Paradoxically, the psychologically most difficult situation seems to be that of professors, despite the flexibility of their time schedules. This is caused by overload, the need to establish and maintain an expertness without formal guidelines, and the difficulty of setting bounds on work.

We tend to think of occupations only in terms of whether they match our talents, our knowledge, and our experiences, and to ignore the fact that they also differ profoundly in terms of the types of lives they allow us to lead. Even people educated in similar ways and with a core of common interests find themselves in occupational roles and organizational settings that represent unexpectedly complicated sets of psychological demands. Hence both individuals *and* organizations must be explicit about the role of occupational demands on private life. The cost of not doing so is vividly portrayed in the following interlude.

Interlude II

Nancy Wright: Success?

Nancy Wright is among the first women to have reached the executive level at a large, progressive, dynamic, and successful company. She is an excellent performer, and the company has rewarded her efforts. She loves her work and has succeeded far more than she ever expected. But now, looking back, she expresses some concerns. Why?*

The Story

Nancy Wright has been with the company for more than fifteen years. She joined it when her previous job with a bank required more travel than she thought she could manage: "I love to travel, thought it was exciting. But as I started to think about planning a family, I realized that having a family plus the amount of traveling I had to do were sort of mutually exclusive." At that

*This case study is based on an interview conducted by Amy Andrews, who contributed greatly to the analysis. It is a stand-alone case, for we have no information from her spouse or her coworkers or managers.

point she was not thinking about a career. "What I really thought about was a job and an interesting job."

Nancy married immediately after college; after five years of work at the bank, when she began to think of having children, she felt that a change made sense. Negotiations took a long time, and by the time she was offered a job at her present company she was pregnant:

> So I turned down the job, saying that it didn't make sense to join [the company] because I was pregnant. . . . The person that I was interviewing with said, "Well, what difference should that make?" I said I really hadn't decided on whether I wanted to work. He said, "Even if you only work at the company six months, I'll feel lucky that we got you for those six months." So I thought, why not? My husband was supportive. . . . So anyway, I wound up joining the company. I was three months pregnant.

Before taking the job, Nancy asked for and got agreement that she could have a three-month leave of absence once the baby was born. Company policy at the time was flexible (though all leave was unpaid), but normally there was a requirement to return to work after eight weeks. About the added leave Nancy said, "I had negotiated that right up front as part of the decision to come. Because, after all, I knew I was pregnant, and I knew my due date and all that."

Nancy was attached to the company because she felt that "the corporate world tended to attract bright, aggressive people, and you tended to get ahead based on your abilities rather than time in the job." It was different from the bank, which was "conservative, not the best and brightest, no fast-track kind of potential—they didn't single people out and deal with them separately. It was sort of a 'wait your turn' environment."

The baby came early, and Nancy worked until the day she delivered. "I came back after three months, and as it turns out, I had a very difficult baby and was more than happy to flee the house and come back to work. I went through some difficult child care arrangement times." She and her husband wanted a live-in au pair, but they had difficulty finding someone who was reliable and would stay. "There just simply wasn't anybody I could turn to. Nobody I knew worked and had children, let along had live-in help." Nancy's parents and in-laws lived in the area but were not very supportive of her going back to work.

> It's not that they were deliberately working against me, but they just felt that my place was home with the baby, that my husband was a successful attorney, what do you need to work for? That was their attitude. Just simply not understanding why, having chosen to have a child, I would choose to go back to work.

Her husband, however, was very supportive: "whatever would make me happy he would be willing to do."

After a particularly harrowing experience with a baby-sitter, and because her father had fallen ill, Nancy almost quit work. But her boss (the same man who had hired her) said, "Why don't you take as much time as you need, get through your father's illness, straighten up the child care situation, and let me know if I can be of help." Nancy took a few weeks off, during which time her father died and her mother-in-law found an older woman to take care of the child.

> It was a very stressful time. . . . It was stressful having a child that was very colicky, very difficult. It was stressful going through all of these rotating baby-sitters . . . and feeling totally inadequate and also feeling that I wasn't doing a good job at work because of all this stress. But anyway, I found a woman, and my husband and I agreed that either it worked this time or I would quit. And it worked! The woman was an older woman, she had raised a number of kids of her own, she needed a job, and she was with us for five and a half years. She, in effect, raised my son and was there when, three and a half years later, I had another child, and brought up that child until she was two.

Nancy nursed the second child, a girl, by going home two to three times a day. And she also had to leave at times to drive her son to preschool, since the caretaker could not drive.

> So there was a period of time, I would say during the first five to six years that I was at the company, that my loyalties were very divided—where my heart wasn't always in my work and I clearly was not giving work my all. . . . Also, shortly after I got the child care situation straightened out, my boss changed. And the second boss was far less sympathetic and far less patient with my coming and going to the house to nurse my daughter or to take my son to preschool or whatever, and he and I really got along very poorly. We were at loggerheads all the time over the time away from the office.

Nonetheless, Nancy was given more and more responsibility, including more travel. During her daughter's first year, Nancy was in Europe seven times (for between one and two weeks each time) and took a trip to the Far East:

> Although there were times where the tradeoff meant my family came first or my responsibilities at home came first, there were also times where I just simply said, so my son can't go to preschool, or he goes in a taxi. Or I get friends to do it. But again, in those days, it was very unusual for a woman to be working, a woman who lived in the suburbs and who had other forms of livelihood. It was unusual.

When the Wrights' caretaker finally left, they got another older woman, who stayed with them for two years. During this time Nancy went off to a residential executive training program, the only woman among more than one hundred men. This program took her out of the home for many weeks except for Saturday night and Sunday. Her husband, who had been consistently supportive until then, found this a difficult period.

I really enjoyed the school experience. [But] for the first time, the trade-off that I was making caused friction between my husband and myself. He could clearly tell that I was enjoying school—I made no secret about it, that I enjoyed being away from home . . . so that I think there may have been some jealousy. There may have been some resentment that there she is, having a great time with all of these guys, and I'm left at home with the burden of the responsibility. . . . I think it didn't help that people said to me—our friends, or people at work, or his family—"Oh, it must be so tough on you being at school." No one said to him, "And look at the wonderful thing you're doing taking care of the home front while she has this great opportunity." Everyone was somehow saying what a tough thing it was for me, and it wasn't at all. I was having a grand old time. I was working hard, but I was having a great time. I think that was, of all the years of work/home trade-off, the most stressful time, because of the fact that my husband's support wasn't really there emotionally. . . . It was a stressful time recovering from it as well. So we went through about a good year of relationship difficulty over the whole thing, which we have weathered and got through.

On the whole, Nancy has had very supportive managers, people with families of their own who understood her needs, "understood that there would be times when I was here 150 percent of what was required and other times when it was only 50 percent of what was required." In part, Nancy educated her managers to be understanding.

I think [I succeeded] mainly because I was in touch with it and confronted them with the fact that there were trade-offs to be made. I wasn't in touch with it in the very beginning, but over time, as I became aware of what was causing me stress, I was able to verbalize it and share it with my manager and able to say "Look, it's 5:30 and I've got to go,". . . or "I'll be in late tomorrow because my daughter's in the school play."

The Wrights still have live-in help, now mainly someone to handle car pools and "cook and keep our life organized and on track—arrange for plumbers, arrange for electricians, that kind of thing. It's not so much primary day care provider any more as it is sort of chief cook and bottle washer."

Nancy has no sense that her family concerns ever put her at a disadvantage at work or in competition with peers. Indeed, she has been extremely successful in her career, and she now has one of the highest positions of any woman in the company. Nor does she feel that being a woman played any part in her career or in the reaction that people had to her. "One of the sort of coping mechanisms that I've had over the years is to not recognize any difference between myself and my male counterparts." So she is the model of the woman who did it all, achieving exceptional things in the professional world and having a family as well. But she is not interested in progressing any further up the ladder or in "moves that would prepare me developmentally for the next promotion or the next assignment," a feeling she has shared with her boss. In fact, she has asked her boss to let her know if he ever wants her to move out of the position she is in, at which point she would probably leave the company.

As Nancy reflects back on her career, things begin to take on a different look. She recognizes that her life has indeed been different from that of her male peers. "I now see that I have had to make trade-offs and I am different in a lot of ways, that women in general are different than men in a lot of ways. I'm more in touch with that now than I used to be. But at the time . . . I didn't think of it that way." She realizes that though she had a family, hers was "not a very demanding home life, or at least a home life where I could pass it off, trade it off without a lot of hassle."

In hindsight, Nancy regrets some of the choices and trade-offs she made. Over the years, she says, she chose to escape into her work. She found it easier to deal with the problems at work than the problems her children had in school. She drew more satisfaction from work and advanced by following the rules of an environment in which children, child care, and parenting were devalued. Indeed, for most of her career the notion of placing family above work was so foreign to her professional world that the choice did not even seem to exist. She did not feel aware of the costs, the long-term implications of her decisions. Despite this, Nancy feels that her decisions were entirely her own. But she does not at this point feel good about them.

If I had it do all over again, I think I would do things very differently. . . . I think I probably would have taken off several years instead of choosing to go right back to work. I think with the benefit of hindsight, which of course is real easy for me to say given my position, the security of having achieved where I am, it's easy to look back and say, "that's how I would do it." I'm not sure I'd have the guts to do it that way, but my relationship with my son to this day is mediocre to poor and I think it's traceable back to [the fact that] I had an escape valve. There were many years in which after dinner—which I didn't eat with the children; the children were always fed before I got home, so I had dinner with my husband—I went up to my study and I sat and did work for the office and I was unavailable for my young children, to play with, to parent, to put to bed, because I was all-consumed with responsibilities at work because I really enjoyed it and I didn't enjoy [and] never had to get used to doing the mothering tasks of reading to them.

I can't even count on one hand the number of times I sat down and read them a book. Or played a game with them. Though I think I have a good relationship with my daughter, it is not the quality of the relationship that I think I would have been enjoying if the foundation had been there for her as a young child, or even as a not-so-young child. . . . I put a lot more of my emotional energy and a lot more of my *self* into work than I did into being a parent.

61

Such a lament has frequently been heard from male executives at a similar stage in their lives, and Nancy has followed a "male" route to career success. But her actions also have implications for women and for the company's hope of achieving gender equity in its management ranks, for she is an active voice inside the company encouraging young mothers to consider taking time off from work to be with their children, and to think hard about the choices they are making. She tells them:

> No one's going to write on my tombstone, "Nancy Wright, senior executive of [company]." Hopefully someone will write on my tombstone, "Loving wife and mother." No one will remember, hopefully, when I die at eighty-five, that I even worked here. But hopefully my children, who I haven't done a real terrific job raising, will get through whatever resentment they feel about that and we will have been able to establish a relationship where they will care to write on my tombstone, "She was a loving mother."

What is complicated about this reaction is that Nancy limits her concerns to the women in the company. She thinks "there should be a place in every company for women to be able to take the slower track for a while, to work part-time, or to take off a couple years, and to be able to come back to work and give of themselves 150 percent of the time once they are through some of those early child-raising years, which are the most demanding timewise." But if one makes special arrangements only for women, it will not be possible to provide gender equity in the work place. Women will have been singled out for needs that make them less fully members of the organization, and the real needs of many men will have been neglected.

Thus Nancy's story illustrates two clear costs that occur when the work organization remains unchanged and individuals self-select into the most ambitious roles. The personal costs are evident; the guilt and self-recrimination Nancy feels are painful. But the organization pays a cost as well. Investing as it does in the training and development of women managers and striving for gender equity at all levels of the organization, the company is now faced with the fact that a woman such as Nancy, who has succeeded by conventional standards and who should be the role model for younger women, is actively encouraging them (and not men) to take time off from work. Because of this, the organization's initiatives toward achieving a more balanced management team are frustrated.

Comment

Is Nancy Wright a success? Yes, but by a narrow set of rules that govern only one part of her life. And paradoxically, the personal cost she has had to pay for this success is now having unintended organizational ramifications. Not only is she herself no longer available for advancement, but her advice to younger women makes their progress problematic. Her well-meaning attempts to alert younger female employees to possible future regret presumes that the issues she faced are only women's issues. By ignoring the role of general workplace demands—or by assuming that these are given and not subject to change—she falls into the "mommy track" view of organizational life. As such, her interventions inadvertently undermine the stated desire of her company to move women into the upper ranks of management. True gender equity requires not special (and inevitably invidious) distinctions, however benignly meant, but general provisions for flexibility in career paths that will benefit men as well as women.

CHAPTER 4

FAMILY AS AN EMERGING ISSUE FOR ORGANIZATIONS

T he story of Nancy Wright highlights some of the personal and organizational costs of current company practices. If successful careers presume singular involvement with work, then private lives will suffer. But as is evident from Nancy Wright's story, such difficulties eventually feed back into organizational concerns. Whether through employee stress and attrition or the loss to top management of the services of significant parts of the work force, companies are also suffering from their traditional expectations.[1]

The price they pay, however, is generally unrecognized. Responses to a recent reorganization intended to make a large and successful manufacturing company more competitive, for example, have led to increased demands on the engineering division. Work hours have increased and meetings are being held on weekends; in general, morale is down and anxiety is up. Unknown to management, a number of the best performers in the division—some recently promoted into positions of increased responsiblity—are thinking of leaving. "I love the company and would like to stay, but I can't sacrifice my family" is a typical comment.

At some level, of course, there is an awareness that the needs of employees' families are affecting their working lives. The overall facts are familiar: in the early 1990s, fewer than 10 percent of families follow the pattern of a husband at work and a wife at home caring for the children.[2] More than half of all mothers with children under the age of one are in the paid labor force,[3] and forty-five percent of all paid workers are women.[4] Of all households, 28 percent are headed by females.[5] Further, 60 percent of men in the labor force are married to wives who also hold jobs.[6] It therefore is not surprising that a study by the Bank Street Work and Family Life staff found that roughly half of all employees are having problems managing the combined demands of jobs and family life.[7] And in a survey based on twelve hundred employees of one large company, 45 percent of the professionals indicated that "my concentration or judgment at work is often affected by my family concerns."[8]

These trends are not likely to reflect a transient phenomenon like the influx of women into the work force during World War II. On the contrary, such changes are projected to be even more dramatic by the end of the century.[9] Since the United States—almost alone among industrialized countries—has no national family policy, and since it is difficult for women by themselves to find a satisfactory solution, the issues seem to be devolving on employing organizations.

Some organizations are beginning to respond. The response has mainly come in the form of new employer-based benefits: parental leave; employee assistance programs (EAPs), originally geared to substance abuse and now more often involved in work-family issues; and help of various kinds with dependent care, including flexible spending accounts, alternative work schedules, and flexible benefits or so-called cafeteria plans.[10]

For example, IBM has added to its already generous family

services (including child and elder care referral services, EAPs, and adoption assistance) two new initiatives: a personal leave program of three years, during which time employees receive company-paid benefits and are assured of a job on returning; and expanded flextime, where employees have the option of starting work up to an hour before or after the normal starting time. The personal leave initiative is accompanied by the option of part-time work during the first year, with the requirement that employees be available for part-time work during the second and third years if their services are needed. Thus employees are given the flexibility they need while ensuring that their ties to the company and its work are not completely severed. For this reason, IBM is also starting a pilot program that will allow employees on personal leave to work at home, as long as the tasks they are assigned are amenable to this arrangement and they agree to come to their workplace at least four consecutive hours during the week.

More recently, the Xerox Corporation introduced what it calls "life cycle assistance," which provides $10,000 worth of benefits to be used at any point in an employee's career. The first benefit provided is a child care subsidy, prorated according to annual salary. Other areas in consideration include housing aid, dependent college tuition, elder care, and partial pay replacement for family leaves. And a new labor contract at AT & T includes a family care package consisting of a fund for the development of community child care centers and services for the elderly, grants to help parents trying to adopt children, and parental and family illness leaves of up to one year with continuation of basic benefits and a guaranteed job at the end.

Unfortunately IBM, Xerox, and AT & T are not representative of all U.S. employers—certainly not of small firms, nor of those with fewer skills requirements or less benevolent attitudes, though similar arrangements on an individual basis are often possible for valued employees in those cases.[11] But since these more enlightened benefits are generally seen as a model for the national response to work-family issues, it is important to subject them to analysis.

The responses of these leading American corporations fall into two general categories. First are benefits in the form of services or financial and information aid in obtaining them—benefits that allow employees with family responsibilities more easily to spend time and energy on work. Such responses are meant to help employees in different family situations and with different needs to fit the procedures originally designed for a more homogeneous work force, one where 100 percent commitment to work and organization could be presumed because an employee either was single or had family support at home. For example, hospitals badly in need of primarily female nursing help, often at irregular hours, frequently provide on-site child care arrangements. And a number of law firms (including the one in which Allen Chase works; see Interlude I) have recently made provision to care for employees' children when they are sick or when normal arrangements break down.

A second category consists of policies that create flexibility in location and time, as well as varying arrangements for personal leave. The aim is to provide employees with more control and discretion over the conditions of work. These benefits include flextime and "flexplace," part-time and job-sharing opportunities, and family and medical leaves. They are geared to freeing time for employees themselves to attend to family needs.

All of these responses are certainly helpful, but they are still based on the assumption that employees' family concerns can be treated on the margins, conceptually distinct from the primary goals of the organization. Though gender neutral by law, they thus are mainly geared to trying to help women manage careers while also caring for their families. Moreover, both sets of responses have unintended negative consequences. Family benefits of the first variety do not help employees gain nonwork time. And since the availability, affordability, and quality of these services are far from adequate, such responses may even increase the work-family concerns facing American workers. They may actually exacerbate the conditions the benefits are designed to alleviate. And as long as organizations continue to reward the full commitment of their employees on the basis of the amount of visible time spent at work, flexibility (even when available) will be seen as a liability for the development of one's career. Such benefits therefore support the separation of work in the public economic arena from that in the private domestic domain, and may create—or reinforce—a two-tier structure of employment.

EXACERBATING FAMILY-WORK PRESSURES

During much of this century the effort to alleviate the pressures of employment have served to reduce the amount of time people spent in the workplace, but recently that trend has been reversed.[12] Since the mid-1970s, work time in the United States has increased 15 percent;[13] among managers the increase is estimated as almost 20 percent during the 1980s.[14] And though most European countries provide longer periods of paid time away from work than does the United States, the example of competitors in the Far East has led a number of analysts to conclude that longer working hours are necessary to bring the United States back to its previous competitive position.[15]

In particular it is the example of Japan that is held up to support this conclusion.[16] And it is also Japan that serves as a model for the more participative and committed form of organization that is now recommended to increase productivity.[17] Such recommendations seem to ignore the Japanese institutional norms that underlie that system, including the role of women as family support and the economic/financial framework that has exchanged employment security for total commitment in the core work force.[18] Neither of these conditions exists in the United States, and it is unlikely that either could be made congruent with contemporary American circumstances. Yet productivity pressures, combined with globalization and increased international competition, have resulted in longer work hours just when increased family demands are also putting greater pressure on employee time.

Much of what we read about the need for organizational transformation in U.S. companies reflects a concern about productivity. More participation, organizations with fewer managerial levels, and more responsibility and authority at lower levels are among the prescribed solutions. All of these changes demand increased commitment from employees, a commitment that tends (according to current rules) to translate into more time and energy spent on paid work. But if the demographic changes of the past few decades have left the family—and children in particular—as vulnerable as many now fear, then the answer is not to provide the conditions for employees to increase their involvement with work. Rather, the need is to find ways to legitimate equal commitment to private concerns and thus to free time for family needs. That is the goal of the second set of benefits the most enlightened employers are now introducing.

CREATING (OR REINFORCING) A TWO-TIER STRUCTURE OF EMPLOYMENT

As noted earlier, these benefits are geared to freeing time for employees themselves to attend to family needs. As such, they seemingly make legitimate a different, more accommodating set of work place requirements. But trouble arises if current cultural assumptions and the organizational procedures that reinforce them remain unchanged. As long as the currently accepted criteria for career success remain, flexibility will not be popular with core employees. Yet dependents will continue to need care. And even though the gendered solution of a specialization of labor between breadwinning and caretaking (which evolved at the Industrial Revolution) is no longer seen as optimal, either economically or psychologically, women still seem to be primarily responsible for care. Thus flexible options are more likely to be used by women than by men.

This difference in patterns of use is likely to increase the disadvantages women already face in the workplace: being overrepresented among the poor, having lower wages than men even when in comparable jobs, and moving more slowly—if at all—

into the higher ranks of organizations. Flexibility superimposed on existing assumptions about the conditions of employment is therefore likely to *increase* gender inequity unless it is accompanied by a reevaluation of the meaning of employment in contemporary American society. Even IBM's response, important as it is, fails to meet this challenge. And the same is true of most other examples of organizational responses to employees' family needs.[20]

By law, U.S. policy in these matters is gender neutral. Pregnancy leave is generally subsumed under disability provisions; custody decisions in divorce cases now favor fathers as well as mothers. But it is not clear that such mandated equality is equitable or that it can overcome the effect of a wage-labor system premised on an ideal of workers without any family responsibilities.[21] Nor is it likely to be equitable in the face of a deeply held cultural assumption that caring is the province of women. Rather, it may force both women and men to choose between economic success without family responsibilities and economic marginalization combined with family care. And it may contribute further to the economic vulnerability of women, as already evidenced by the differential consequences of divorce for men and women in a "gender-neutral" world.[22]

These benefits therefore may entail a cost as long as women are the only ones culturally, psychologically, and economically available to take advantage of them. In order for *all* employees to feel free to use the flexibilities provided, it will be necessary to link work-family issues systemically to organizational change and not deal with them in a piecemeal fashion. These issues must be accepted as an integral part of organizational life and as an important business concern.[23]

Not that any of this is easy. The cultural assumption of the separation of spheres is deeply embedded in our thinking, and organizational structures and practices are anchored in it. As many companies are finding out, cultural change in any case is extremely difficult,[24] and the difficulty is exacerbated when it includes the attempt to bridge this divide. Several teams of researchers, with support from the Ford Foundation, are currently working with companies to reconsider the way they think about work in order to help them be productive and competitive and still allow their employees to meet their personal needs. Though the results of this effort are not yet known, these researchers have discovered how difficult it is for company officials even to agree that employees' personal lives are or should be of concern to their employers. As a member of the human resource department at one of these companies explained: "For over a decade, we have tried to teach managers to *ignore* employees' private circumstances. So it's not easy to get them to think about these issues in a different way."

But economic, social, and demographic changes will force American organizations to come to terms with the needs of their employees' families. In the future, it will no longer be possible to fall back on the assumption that family issues are individuals' private concerns, since the costs of this assumption are becoming increasingly evident. Short-run costs include the potential for increased stress on employees, which has repercussions for both individual and organizational well-being and effectiveness. In the long run, the pressures on dependent care today (particularly of children) may create significant problems in the future for the economy and for society. What is less evident are the consequences, both intended and unintended, of the responses that companies are currently making to these problems. They stem from the fact that work is still designed as if employment and personal life could be neatly divided into separate public and private spheres, with men given the sole responsibility for economic roles and women being responsible for the private family roles. As long as a society distributes its people neatly into cells 1 and 4 of Figure 4–1, the work of both the private and the public domains can be accomplished without social disruption. But with the massive movement of women into the work force, this distribution breaks down.

How are other countries responding to these trends (which are, after all, worldwide)? Different countries have different social infrastructures to deal with family needs, and they are ideologically at different places concerning family roles and gender equity. A cultural comparison therefore allows one to assess the

	HOME (Domestic Sphere)	PAID WORK (Public Sphere)
FEMALE	cell 1	cell 2
MALE	cell 3	cell 4

Figure 4–1

implications of different ways of dealing with these issues. The comparison below is based on the responses of the United States, Great Britain, and Sweden.[25] These are all Western industrialized countries that to a certain extent share a common heritage, yet there are instructive differences in their approach to these concerns.

THE AMERICAN RESPONSE

The United States differs from Great Britain and Sweden both ideologically and institutionally. Both differences are anchored in the following cultural assumptions:[26]

1. Families/children are in the private domain. The choice to have children is entirely personal and should neither be encouraged nor discouraged. Hence any kind of government help in this area is seen as a stigma, a sign of personal failure.

2. The care of children and elders is rightfully the province of women, either because they do it better or because it is somehow their specific job.

3. In an individualistic, achieving society, balance between work and personal life is not seen as a high-priority goal. Career and work success are more important.

Given this set of assumptions, as well as the fact that more than 50 percent of American women (even those with very young

	HOME (Domestic Sphere)	PAID WORK (Public Sphere)
FEMALE	cell 1	cell 2
MALE	cell 3	cell 4

Figure 4–2

children) are now in the work force, the pressure in the United States is on caretaking.[27]

What we have at the moment in the United States is a movement of women into public arenas, thus creating problems for the private sphere. American women at the upper end of the educational and occupational scale are blurring the distinction between male and female occupational roles and accepting work and career as a prime priority.[28] For some women, this strategy is accompanied by a decision not to have children. But even if children are present, we know from detailed case studies (including the Chases and Nancy Wright in Interludes I and II) that according to current career rules, one's family needs to be invisible at work. Women are welcome and indeed desired in influential organizational positions, as long as they follow the rules established for men with traditional family support. But under these conditions, especially in a society that values the public economic world over the private, family and caretaking will necessarily suffer. The situation is summarized in Figure 4–2, which shows that in the United States only one boundary—between male and female work roles—is becoming permeable.

THE BRITISH RESPONSE

The United Kingdom has a more universal social infrastructure; health care and other basic family needs are taken care of independent of employment status. In contrast to the United States, there is also not (as of the early 1990s) the same underlying ideology of equality. On the whole, educated women in Britain are less likely to be caught in the kind of ambivalence that now confronts Nancy Wright. More of them are willing to acknowledge the overriding importance of their family and to accommodate their careers to that priority. And organizations, because they are not responsible for basic social needs, have more leeway in responding to family concerns.

Britain, for example, has for a long time had more institutionalized working-from-home arrangements than most other countries.[29] One British manufacturing company has had a home-based systems development group for more than twenty years. Originally established to retain women with scarce technical skills, it has evolved into a profit-making business unit including men as well as women. Most employees still work part-time, and all spend time away from home at client and office sites. But their base is at home, which gives them control over their time and over the way they do their work. When compared to systems developers in the same company doing their work from an office base, the home-based workers are more loyal and less likely to want to leave the organization, more involved in training and keeping up their skills, less concerned about position and pay, and more satisfied with their personal relations, their health, and the balance of their lives.[30]

More recently, a number of British companies, primarily banks, have introduced a "career breaks" scheme designed to allow higher-level employees to take unpaid leave of from two to five years, with some provision for keeping in touch and with a guaranteed reinstatement at the end of the leave.[31] In some cases there is also an accompanying commitment to negotiate more flexible working arrangements.

Though legally gender neutral, both responses are primarily for women. The changed working arrangements are meant to accommodate the needs of women with children. The result is a reaffirmation, to a certain extent, of the gendered differentiation of spheres. British women can work, but they do so on a

	HOME (Domestic Sphere)	PAID WORK (Public Sphere)
FEMALE	cell 1 ←	cell 2
MALE	cell 3	cell 4

Figure 4-3

"mommy track," which means a continuation of male domination in the workplace. Figure 4–3, which summarizes this response, again shows only one boundary being affected: that between home and paid work for women.

THE SWEDISH RESPONSE

In Sweden the issue is anchored in a very different set of cultural assumptions. Sweden has for almost two decades been committed to equality between men and women, who "are to have the same rights, obligations, and opportunities in all of the main fields of life." This combines with a basic commitment to economic self-sufficiency: the belief that "every individual should have a job paid sufficiently to enable her or him to earn a living."[32] In other words, on the ideological level there is a social consensus in Sweden that women should have jobs and that fathers should be involved in the care of their children. And there is legislation to support both these aims. For example, even though Swedish tax returns are individual, there are certain tax benefits for couples where the woman earns as much as her husband.[33]

Further, the care of families is seen as within the responsibilities of the state. Children in particular are considered a public good, and their proper care is viewed as essential for the continuing success of the society. This has meant not only an elaborate state-supported day care system, but also support for parents to stay home with infants. Parental leave, which is available to both parents (though not at the same time), is reimbursed at 90 percent of salary for twelve months. Parents of young children have the right to work only six hours a day, and there is ample leave for time off when a child is sick.[34]

Thus the Swedish government has mandated a comprehensive set of family policies and has tried hard to change social attitudes. As opposed to the United States, where the effort has been to allow women to meet male work demands, and to Britain, where the emphasis has been on accommodating work to the needs of mothers, the effort in Sweden has been to try to equalize gender roles. Balance between work and family is encouraged for both men and women; men are urged to be more involved in the family and are supported in this effort.

Sweden, as Figure 4–4 points out, is working at three boundaries. Swedish women have an easier time combining the conflicting demands of work and family and show less feelings of conflict and guilt than we see in the United States, and Swedish men find it more ideologically appropriate to spend time at home. But the response is selective, since career rules for moving up in industrial organizations have not changed significantly. Women are seldom found in top positions, and there is even more occupational segregation by sex in Sweden than there is in the United States.[35] Despite much social change, the boundary between men and women in the public sphere is still firm.

These national differences indicate the complexity of women's adaptation and change in the face of changing circum-

	HOME (Domestic Sphere)	PAID WORK (Public Sphere)
FEMALE	cell 1 →	cell 2
MALE	cell 3 ←	cell 4

Figure 4-4

stances. They also make clear that gender is closely linked to the public/private divide, though the way that this gets worked out is highly dependent on the larger social context and on the assumptions underlying the current structure of the workplace.[36]

CONCLUDING NOTE

An interesting analysis of the American situation has recently concluded that the present design of work is, in the legal sense, discriminatory.[37] The argument states that many presumed requirements of high-level work in this country are actually not job related but merely "corporate convenient." For example, long hours or excessive travel may not actually be necessary for a given task; there may be other ways to get the work done. But it is more convenient to continue to impose these "requirements" than to rethink what is actually necessary for the task at hand. The trouble arises because such demands are prejudicial to one particular group—namely, women. It is this combination that fits the legal definition of discrimination.

So what is the answer? How can a society support the work of both the public and the private sphere and at the same time maintain a competitive position and create equity between men and women? Changing underlying values and introducing supportive national policy, as the Swedish example shows, is not sufficient. A change in career rules is also necessary, particularly in those that govern movement to the top of our organizations. More than anything else, we need to reexamine the assumptions we have about the role of time in the evaluation and development of high-level careers.[38]

For too long it has been assumed that long hours equate with productivity, an assumption anchored in assembly line work. But knowledge work, which is increasingly the object of career development efforts, is different.[39] Here the goal could be to work smart, not long; long hours could be seen less as an indicator of commitment and performance than as a sign of inefficiency. Nor is "face time"—visible time at work—any longer a valid basis for the judgment of high performance in an era of communication and information technology.

In general, given current circumstances, it seems necessary to introduce much more differentiation into our thinking about careers.[40] People differ in their needs, and these requirements change over a lifetime. Career rules must reflect these distinctions and discontinuities, or they will not serve the needs of either organizations or their employees. In short, we must deal simultaneously with all four boundaries shown in Figure 4–1.

But why, one may ask, should companies change away from what is habitual and convenient? Legal pressure is one reason. As in the government case against AT & T that resulted in the famous "consent decree," the law can make a dramatic difference.[41] But as I hope to suggest in the final chapters, a company's self-interest may also be at stake, at least when considered in the long term and not merely from the point of view of the next quarterly returns.

CHAPTER 5

RETHINKING TIME AND AUTONOMY

T ime is perhaps the most critical issue in the ability to integrate one's private and public lives.[1] But time is also the traditional way to structure and control work. Managers expect to see their employees at work during a particular period of the day, and they often use time as one of the criteria for the evaluation of performance. To them, time and productivity are closely linked.[2]

The evidence, however, is more complicated. The study referred to in Chapter 4 comparing home-based with office-based systems developers[3] found a higher degree of responsibility for work in the home-based group, a difference attributed by these employees to the greater control they had over their time. The home-based pattern of work was associated with greater productivity and increased satisfaction not because of location but because of the way it freed work from the constraints of time as traditionally conceived. Further, one-quarter of the office-based employees indicated that their most productive time was outside the traditional office day, a period that was lost to the company. In contrast, those based at home could work at their individually optimal times and could make use of small bits of available time. One home-based systems developer, recently promoted to management, was struck by the greater efficiency of work at home: "Anyone who is working 25 hours a week at home is producing as much good quality output as anyone working full-time in an office. When I do go to offices, I am sometimes appalled by the pure, utter and absolute waste of time that goes on."[4]

Employee control over time, however, is not easy for management to accept. The strength of traditional beliefs is evident even in a forward-looking and enlightened personnel manager who made it clear that he would not mind at all having one of his trusted subordinates spend a day working from home. But then he added, "Of course, if there were an important game on TV, I might be tempted to check and see whether he was working!" The notion of adjusting work time to personal concerns was still foreign to him, even though the employee would probably be more productive if he could watch the game, then do the work when there would be nothing to compete for his concentration.[5]

There also are other, more specific potential advantages of more individualized patterns in the timing of work. Work in off-hours takes advantage of periods of low computer utilitization or of times in different parts of the world. If accepted as legitimate, such patterns might also be cheaper. Thus the critical work of one unit of mainframe support people had to be done during night shifts to reduce the interference with the daily use of the computer. Nonetheless, these employees were still expected to be in the office during the normal workday—where they sat around and talked, because there were no real tasks for them to do—and then they were given overtime for off-shift duty.

Over and over again one hears how time permeates the

management of work. "The culture is that you get credit for long hours. Working long hours is the thing to do. There is no forty-hour week; if you are not doing at least fifty, you are not a team player. It's a sign of dedication, [and it] doesn't matter if there's work to do."[6] Time is also viewed as infinitely available. "The only way to attack the problem is with hours and hours of work." And only people who put in the time are seen as slated for career success. "It's not that someone who doesn't is seen as not being a good performer, but they are not seen as aggressive in wanting to move up in the company." And so, in general, they don't.

The underlying assumption seems to be that employee time belongs to the company, a notion reinforced by the company's evaluation and promotion practices. Yet other voices acknowledge the irrationality of this cultural norm: "If there are two people of equal performance, the promotion will go to the one who has put in the overtime. But that means it took that person longer to get the same level of performance, so the other guy is the better one. It makes no sense."

Time, of course, is not infinite; it is a scarce and rather precious resource, particularly for those whose involvements and responsibilities extend beyond the sphere of work.[7] But as long as the amount of time spent at work is seen as a prime indicator of commitment and productivity, the emphasis on long hours will remain. And this, particularly when rigidly prescribed, is a key element in the inability to meet conflicting responsibilities. One young male assistant professor reported that "the [university's] expectations about one's commitment to individual career—to the exclusion of spouse's career and family—make it virtually impossible to live a life in which personal goals can be considered (much less accomplished) apart from work." At that same university, two out of five young faculty members who were parents noted that they had seriously considered leaving because of time conflicts between family and work. It is therefore important to probe beneath the surface meaning of time, to go beyond flextime and leaves—important as these are—to reach a deeper understanding of the role of time in people's work lives.

For many people, the structuring of time provided by work and occupation is central to their sense of reality. Studies of unemployment have shown how disruptive to the structure of life is an "everlasting present" with no sense of past or future. In that situation, only people with an unusually well-developed internal sense of structure know how to use the endless time made available.[8] These results presume that only work provides the structure of a person's life, but one can well argue that the totality of life's demands can provide this inner sense of direction. The systems developers who worked from their homes were not dependent on their employers or customers to provide structure or social contact; they received these supports from their families and communities.

From the organizational point of view also, a different conception of time need not be detrimental. We know from Parkinson that work expands to fill the time available. Psychological experiments have shown that people will complete the same tasks in very different amounts of time, depending on the initial time allotments they are given.[9] Experiments have also shown that if time is constrained, work that must get done will be fitted into whatever time is available.[10] In one small computer company, for example, the employees found their work expanding to a longer and longer day. The company was small and informal enough, and the employees close enough to the owner, for them simply to inform him that they would no longer work past 5:00 P.M. Surprisingly, there was no unfinished business at the end of their new days.[11] They managed to do the same amount of work in less time once they themselves had control over this aspect of their work. Time as a proxy indicator of performance would actually have distorted the goals of efficient production that such an evaluation would be meant to further.[12]

A female technical manager from a large company observed a similar phenomenon in her engineering division:

> Women work harder to be more efficient. Men just plug away, they just work harder and longer but in the same old way. I don't see in men that they think, "OK, I have sixty

hours of work and forty-five hours in which to do it—how can I accomplish this?" Instead, they just muscle through. Women want to keep the quality standard but find ways to do it smarter.

This observation is a comment less on any essential difference between the sexes than on what is possible when time is viewed as constrained rather than infinite, when long hours are seen as a sign of *in*efficiency rather than of commitment and motivation. For example, Jack Welch, the CEO of General Electric, is reported to have said that anyone who cannot do his job in forty hours is not doing it right. So one can work hard to be efficient—what is often referred to as working smart—or work long hours. The difference is critical to the ability of employees to mesh their work responsibilities with the needs of their private lives.

The effort of the "smart" workers, however, often goes unrecognized. As the technical manager quoted above said, "they do their own work smarter, but that is not enough to change the process." By *process*, this manager meant the underlying cultural assumptions about time. No matter how efficient a person may be, the expected amount of time at work remains the same. As one manager put it, "with 20 percent more efficiency, I could function with 20 percent fewer people." It seems that what managers would really like is for employees to work smart *and* long, which they think would either increase output or enable fewer people to perform the current level of work. We compare ourselves to Japan, where employees are seen as more efficient and to work even longer hours, instead of to Germany, where the workweek is considerably shorter than in the United States.[13]

Such reasoning rests on an assumed linear relationship between time and productivity. This may be true for a machine but not for people, especially not knowledge workers. People may be able to work smart for limited periods of time, but not for long hours; fatigue, attention span, and concern over other needs not being met all preclude this simple linear relationship. There is no mystery in any of this. It is obvious from anyone's personal perspective, and is corroborated also by research that indicates that part-time work and job sharing increase productivity per hour worked.[14]

Yet there is an underlying assumption in American companies that fewer people doing more work will increase productivity. American, as opposed to German, industry has created a divisive distinction between people who have been laid off and the survivors, who spend more and more time on the remaining work.[15] The alternative of having more people work less time (through permanent part-time arrangements or job sharing, for example) is often seen as unworkable. To be sure, there are aspects of U.S. policy that make it an economical choice to treat people as a cost rather than as an asset to be deployed in the most effective way. American companies are constrained because they are responsible for basic benefits such as health insurance, which means that the return on this cost is greater if each employee so covered does a greater proportion of the required work. And the tax structure also plays a role. For example, if a $100,000 job is held by one professional, the company pays social security tax on only half this salary. But if the same job were to be shared by two people, the company would have to pay this tax on the whole salary.

Ideally, therefore, one would want social legislation that would not be constraining on different and more innovative ways for companies to deal with their employees' time. But even without such change, there are isolated examples of a different approach. Some companies are beginning to have an approach to employee time that is much more flexible than the shift of an hour or so represented by most flextime programs. The Starbucks Coffee Company based in Seattle, for example, has many part-time workers. It views its employees as its main assets and provides a benefit plan for all that includes health insurance, pension, and stock options."[16] And the human resource director of Microsoft reports that its employees are free to come and go, to take time "to play squash with a spouse or meet with a child's teacher":

In most companies it's the rule to have everybody on site from 8:00 A.M. to 5:00 P.M.; here, it's the exception. We have no set hours. Because every employee has an E-mail account, this significantly reduces the number of meetings, memos, and conferences that are normally required in a more traditional workplace. It's an unstructured atmosphere where work groups are project-oriented. They move and change as needed to get the job done. We trust our employees' judgment in terms of when they're here or working at home as long as the job gets done.[17]

Other companies are defining time in new ways. Arthur Andersen, the accounting firm, has recently received an award from Catalyst, a nonprofit research organization that works with business to enhance the position of women. The company was cited for a policy that allows employees "to cut back to half-time for up to three years and return with compensatory time to reenter the competition for partnership." And the definition of half-time in this policy was not "half the number of hours, but . . . half the client load—a measure of productivity rather than simply of time."[18]

But these examples are still exceptions. Rather than organizing work around the needs of the task, in most American companies the work gets organized by means of the cultural expectations surrounding time. Time at work responds to the clock, instead of to the task; somehow one must always be at work, even when the job may not require it. So there is overwork at the same time as there is slack, and there is little attempt to differentiate between tasks that are urgent and those that are not.

Moreover, the beginning and ending time of the workday seems to be the critical indicator. Employees in one company, in contrast to those at Microsoft, reported that exercising from 12:00 to 1:30 P.M. in an 8:00-to-6:00 day is considered more time at work than working through to 4:30 P.M. and then exercising. This company was very responsive to employees' needs on an emergency basis, but the legitimacy of ordinary needs was missing. One might call this the Ross Perot syndrome: he has been described as someone who will send a jet to fetch a doctor for a sick child but will not take seriously the desire of an employee to be home at Christmas.[19]

Since time is one of the easiest aspects of work to measure precisely, it pervades the mechanisms of evaluation and control. Perin found that managers who were unwilling to let professional employees work at home during the regular workday had no difficulty with *overtime* work at home.[20] Such spillover extends managerial control into private life; the work-at-home pattern during normal hours undermines this control. And so organizational tasks are subordinated to time, instead of time responding to the requirements of the work and of individual circumstance.[21]

External time constraints create a rigidity that interferes with effective performance, as well as with the ability of employees to act on their commitments to both family and work. Even professionals who seemingly have control over their own time and whose work appears to be task-based are caught in this dilemma. As was evident in Chapter 3, the seeming temporal autonomy provided for professors creates an atmosphere of constant availability that presumes a hierarchy of commitments where occupational demands necessarily take precedence over those of family.

Ironically, the dilemma that temporal autonomy creates for professionals has led to efforts to specify in contractual terms exactly what is expected of them and when. This may ease total time demands, but it changes the psychological contract between professionals and their employing organizations. As Starkey notes in his analysis of British teachers, the decreased discretion over the use of their time has led to their "withdrawal of good will"—of doing things for the sake of the students rather than because they are prescribed by contract.[22] As in other control systems, careful specification of terms tends to drive work toward the lowest acceptable level of performance.

Thus time represents a cultural category associated with a number of strongly held beliefs. These place greater value on employment time than on private time, and they presume that time spent on a job is a valid indicator of dedication and performance. Such beliefs are reinforced by assumptions about managerial control and by national policy that holds employers responsible for much of social welfare.

Finally, two observations about current managerial practices and how they affect the issues surrounding employee time: the first relates to flexibility, broadly defined; the second to empowerment. In both cases, company goals and workers' concerns *could* be linked, as long as personal time is seen as a legitimate employee need.

Current thinking about more productive work organizations introduces flexibility in many areas. Management wants employees to respond to tasks rather than to rigid routines; employees want work to be responsive to life needs. Management wants flexibility for productivity reasons, but wants to control it; for personal concerns, employees need to be able to control their own conditions of work. Such desires, though seemingly divergent, are not necessarily contradictory. They can be linked if the following are accepted and taken for granted:

1. There is a diversity of organizational tasks, each with different real demands of presence and time.

2. There is a diversity of individual needs, based on personal circumstances and changing as these circumstances change.

3. There exists technology to manage the logistics of linking the two sets of needs.

Office secretaries, for example, are said to have to be present from 9:00 A.M. to 5:00 P.M. in order to answer the phones. But new phone systems, with voice mail and call forwarding, allow the task of responding to calls to be handled in a different way. Flexible arrangements would not be difficult to establish so long as the secretary's right to control personal time is accepted as a legitimate part of the organization of work.

By attempting to improve productivity through a quicker response to changing conditions and greater commitment and motivation of employees, American companies are trying to move discretion and authority down to the level of those actually doing the work. What has come to be known as "empowerment" is the goal, and leading companies are striving to understand what this means and how to introduce it. It is a problem for managers, whose role in an empowered environment is far from clear. They will have to change from control to support, from setting procedures and monitoring their use to fighting battles for resources and managing coordination with other units. And they will have to learn to think in new ways about time.

Workers in this new environment—particularly professional employees—must also reconsider their role. They are being asked to take more control over their work, to rethink the way they do things, and to eliminate everything that does not add value.[23] If they are successful, they will be able to accomplish more in less time, thus increasing the productivity of the firm. But there will be little incentive to take this mandate seriously if the time that is saved is used either to cut down the work force or to add more work to employees' schedules. At a minimum there should be some explicit expectation that the time saved by the increase in efficiency is shared between employees and the company.

Other Meanings of Time

In a global and highly competitive industrial environment, time becomes something to worry about. And time has entered the recent business literature. There is danger, however, in not clearly differentiating between time at the level of organizational systems and time as it affects the individual employee.

TIME AS THE LAST FRONTIER

In a world of multinational corporations and global markets, time arrangements are fluid. An office day in one part of the world is private time elsewhere, and the communication between them can now be instantaneous. Hence time becomes more complicated in ways that analysts in the field of time geography can explain. One analyst, Murray Melbin, has called time the last big frontier, and he talks about the colonization of time: "The last great frontier of human migration is occurring in time—a spreading of wakeful activity throughout the twenty-four hours of the day."[24] The danger here is that the notion of spreading activity over more hours will be applied to the individual employee, instead of to the enterprise as a whole.

TIME AS MONEY

At first glance, this would seem to be a recognition of the scarcity and hence the value of time. But when applied to professional situations (such as those of consultants or lawyers) where billing is by the hour, the danger is that it leads to longer hours rather than toward more efficient performance.

TIME TO MARKET

Most American product companies are concerned with decreasing the time that it takes a new product to reach the market. Though seemingly unrelated, this notion is often translated into individual hours at work, as in the comments of a high-level product manager: "You hope you have people who can stay day and night to get it done, people who live and breathe engineering design, who don't know enough to go home." But there is no guarantee that time to market can be reduced by employees not going home.

TIME AS A COMPETITIVE ADVANTAGE

This view is a more encompassing notion of the same idea: "As a strategic weapon, time is the equivalent of money, productivity, quality, even innovation."[25] The argument continues with a plea to take time seriously and to track it in the same way as revenues or costs. Again, this is a useful idea at the level of the enterprise, but not if translated into an increased emphasis on individual time at work.

All of these conceptions primarily argue for a shortening of system time, but if they lead in practice to individuals spending more personal time at work, they may have unintended negative consequences. This conflation of system time with personal time may explain some of the unproductive pressure that U.S. companies put on the work time of their employees.

AUTONOMY AND CONTROL

Employees in the administrative division of one large company are currently trying to learn how to let time and location of work be solely determined by the needs of the task, rather than by management decree or traditional cultural expectations. They hope in this way to stay productive and still meet their family needs. Management also sees this as a first attempt to create an empowered work team. The difficulty in such a change is that both managers and work team members need to revise their notions of control and autonomy.

For this attempt to succeed, the role of management would be to lay out the business goals that need to be reached. Within these broad outlines, employees would define the operations and conditions necessary to reach them. Managers would change their role from overseeing the conditions of work to setting the boundaries within which work teams would make their own decisions on who is to work, when, and where.

The problem is that managers may feel that by providing for employee discretion over the use of time, they are giving up all control. Actually, however, they are only asked to give up operational control; workers are asked to be more autonomous, but only on the operational level. Managers need to give clear strategic goals, but employees should be able to decide how best to meet them. Such autonomy has been shown to enhance motivation.[26] It is also necessary for employees to be able to link their company work with private concerns.

Managers would need to be clear about what needs to be accomplished without setting boundaries that are too tightly constraining. It is not an abdication of control (in the sense of letting go completely and leaving workers to fend for themselves) but a clearer demarcation of what is to be controlled by whom: managers control the goals, and employees control the means to reach them.

A good example of how a lack of clear distinction between strategic and operational control can negatively affect both employees and the organization stems from a study of R & D labs.[27] These labs hire professionals, usually from the top university graduates. They feel that these employees desire and deserve autonomy, but they apply it at the wrong point by assuming that industrial R & D employees, like their academic counterparts, need the freedom to set their own problems. Once recruits are established in the lab, however, controls are imposed in an effort to ensure that the actual work done will contribute to business goals. Managers are responsible for organizationally relevant results. When they do not give clear assignments because of the presumed need for an autonomous environment, they are then inclined to apply controls at the level of implementation. Thus, while seemingly providing strategic autonomy (the freedom to set one's own research direction), they withhold operational autonomy (the discretion to decide how to pursue this goal).

But this is *not* what these employees want, and the combination of strategic autonomy with operational control was found to detract from the performance of these workers. In fact, the highest performers in one large central R & D lab were found among those who had started their work in the lab with the lowest strategic autonomy. Managers, therefore, need not fear a total loss of control; on the contrary, they must retain strategic control.

These conclusions are supported by other studies of research scientists.[28] Toren, in altogether different national cultures, looked at four possible areas of autonomy: two core areas, project selection (strategic) and methods selection (operational); and two ancillary areas, budget allocation and selection of coworkers. She found that in two quite different national cultures (Soviet and American), the order of preference for autonomy in these four areas was the same. First came control over methods (operational autonomy), followed by coworker selection; project selection (strategic autonomy) was third in both groups. And Garden, in a study of software professionals in English high-tech companies, reported that her productive people needed initial guidance on objectives and then wanted to be "left alone to get on with it."[29]

What is important to employees is operational autonomy, or the control over the conditions of work. Such control reflects the psychological need to have some say over one's immediate environment, and it is an area that has already been suggested as usefully left in employees' own hands.[30] But particularly in high-level work where results are not easily measurable, specification of these conditions is often seen by managers as a way to maintain control over the work process. Management by walking around—by overseeing the way subordinates work—is part of the received wisdom of how to manage, and it is hard for managers to relinquish it. Yet such a change could be beneficial for all.

Consider the introduction of computer-aided design (CAD) in a large consumer products company. Managers were used to monitoring the work of their subordinates, who had been seated around a large drafting table, by overseeing the process by which they arrived at their designs. But once these design engineers were huddled over individual computer screens, this control over process was no longer possible. The managers became uncomfortable: the screen was too small for two people, and it contained more detail than could be seen as a whole. This forced supervisors to shift their attention to the output, which appeared as a printout two floors below the design floor, and away from the process by which the design was created. They had to relinquish some control and had to be more trusting of the competence of their subordinates. The designers gained autonomy at the operational level, but the supervisor had to change the mode of managing and had to be clearer about the specifications of the final product.

Similarly, when Rank Xerox started its networking experiment in 1982, the company closed one of its buildings and over the next four years set up about 5 percent (fifty men and six women) of the central office staff as independent businesses working out of their homes.[31] These people were in computer systems development, marketing, market research, business planning, finance, law, tax accounting, personnel (recruitment, safety, security, and pensions), and public relations. The company was very careful about its initial selection of networkers. Choices were based in part on personality tests; the company refused to take anyone with high social needs. Having made its selections, Rank Xerox then helped these people set up their own companies. It provided them with the computer equipment they needed; trained them in sales techniques, taxation, and other issues of small businesses; counseled them and their families on the problems associated with an office at home (even having outside consultants design various alternative home set-ups); and contracted for their services up to 50 percent of their total output.

Of particular importance is the company's claim that this 50 percent was equivalent to the full-time services of these people when they were office based. Rank Xerox attributed this, first, to an increase in productivity of the networkers when they were working on their own and for themselves (the advantage of autonomy). Second, management techniques were improved, because it became necessary for managers of the networkers to make closer specifications of need and to think more precisely about the standards that the work had to meet (a change in the definition of managerial control).

It is interesting to note that in retrospect the company felt that its biggest mistake was too great a concentration of concern on the networkers and not enough on their managers. These managers needed new skills in organizing output: designing and scheduling of work, setting quality standards, and coordinating input from a dispersed work force. To manage this, they had to learn not to be concerned with *how* things were done. It was a set-up that had to be based on operational autonomy for the employees, and it benefited both them and the company.

The value of shifting from focusing on input (time put in, way of working) to focusing on output (the results of work) is not a new idea, but it is difficult for many managers to accept. Garden confronted a manager with complaints from his software staff that they felt "completely shackled by their boss's detailed control." "I know it doesn't work well," he replied, "but I can't help myself."[32] Ironically, such a change in managerial behavior is actually easier when people are on their own and *not* visible. As one manager put it:

> If they are near one is more critical and everyone is different. If you see them, you see how they are working. If they are remote you only look at the end result, and that is an advantage. . . . When someone is at hand, you bother them more than necessary, [but] if they're away one doesn't trouble; therefore one would deal only with the more important things.

Thus the need of employees to have operational autonomy requires managers to substitute a basic trust (in terms of both competence and effort) for direct surveillance and control. It has been said, for example, that the reason Sweden does not worry about employees misusing the sixty days per year they are allowed to take off for illness of children (the actual average is between six and seven) is a strong belief in their sense of fairness and commitment.[33] Yet American (and British) managers seem to assume that if one does not see one's subordinates working, they probably are not.

In interviews exploring the possibility of using computers to work at home during the regular workweek on tasks that require cognitive concentration, Perin again and again heard managers asking, "How do I know he's working if I don't see him?" And yet they had no answer to the responding question: "How do you know he's working when you *do* see him?"[34] It is only a managerial assumption that one must control the work process of one's employees. With changes in technology and the growing interdependence of work, a transformation in this mode of managing may be necessary in any case. Operational autonomy at the working level may be required for organizational adaptation to a rapidly changing environment, and it certainly will help individuals trying to mesh work and family concerns.

Technology can enable and support such a transformation of work. The ability to loosen constraints on location is a prime example of technology's potential for effecting change that would also ease workplace limits on accommodations between work and family. For example, the task of writing a technical manual for a large consumer products manufacturer usually took about six months and required the efforts of people separated both geographically and functionally. Once an experimental network was introduced that connected these people electronically, the time to complete the task was cut to less than two months, with no change in quality. One of the people involved quietly took his computer home, and the other members of the group were not even aware that he had changed his location. Thus operational autonomy need not present a dilemma to organizations if certain basic managerial assumptions can be relinquished. But it is difficult to convince supervisors that such arrangements are tenable, since they conflict with basic cultural beliefs about control, the separation of public and private spheres, and time.

Concluding Note

We have seen that operational autonomy—discretion over the conditions of work—is critical to satisfactory and productive work as well as to the ability of employees to satisfy both work requirements and private demands. The most important aspect of this autonomy is the control over time. But if temporal autonomy is combined with demands for constant availability and a primary commitment to occupational work, its potential advantage is nullified. True flexibility of time flows from a basic belief in the legitimacy of a balance of commitments between the private and public spheres.[35]

Nor is it possible for American companies to move toward empowerment—fewer levels of management, more rapid decisions, and coordinated interdependence by means of teams—unless they rethink their beliefs about control. Only if a significant degree of operational control is relinquished by managers will true empowerment be possible, and only if employees' operational autonomy includes control over their time will their needs be met. Such a basic change is necessary to meet the productivity needs of the nation without either returning to a gendered differentiation of economic and domestic arenas or depriving the next generation of the care they need to become a productive work force in their own right.

The cultural barriers to this way of thinking about autonomy and time are clearly evident in the story of Elizabeth Gray, which follows in Interlude III.

Interlude III

Elizabeth Gray: Failure?

*E*lizabeth Gray works in a progressive company, a company that prides itself on giving its employees great flexibility in their work. Yet when Elizabeth wanted to arrange a part-time schedule after the birth of her child, the negotiations collapsed. Why?*

The Story

Elizabeth Gray graduated from business school in 1983. Interested in both marketing and human resources, she took a position in the internal management consulting group of a rapidly growing, innovative company. While she was drawn to the organization for geographic and job content reasons, she was

*This case study is written jointly with Amy Andrews. The story is based on her interviews and her analysis of the situation. See Amy Andrews, *Flexible working schedules in high commitment organizations: A challenge to the emotional norms?*, Sloan School of Management Working Paper #3329-91-BPS, MIT, 1991.

also impressed by the stated human resources philosophy of the company. It was a company that valued diversity, valued its employees, and actively sought ways to create an environment in which employees could perform at peak capacity.

Elizabeth worked in the management consulting group for two and a half years. She was a strong performer, earning the respect and trust of her clients in the organization. A high-level executive in the marketing group was particularly impressed with her talent and brought her into his group in early 1986. When he left the company only a few months later, he asked Carol Peters, his colleague, to provide Elizabeth with the mentoring and guidance she needed.

Elizabeth worked in this group for about a year, but it was a difficult and unsettling year. First, both of the women with whom she was mostly associated—Carol Peters and Susan Carey—were absent on maternity leave during her first summer, leaving Elizabeth with a somewhat vague set of reporting relationships in a new work group. Second, Elizabeth herself became pregnant in the spring of the same year. Carol and Susan returned to work full-time in the fall, and Elizabeth left (two weeks early) at Thanksgiving. When she left, Elizabeth expected to return to a full-time position; as the time neared to return, however, she decided a part-time schedule made more sense. In the following spring, the three women tried to work out an arrangement whereby Elizabeth could administer the program she had previously run, but now on a part-time basis.

Elizabeth's husband Mark fully supported her decision to return to work. They had met in college. After graduation, Mark worked in retail before taking a position with a government agency. When he and Elizabeth decided to get married, they moved to the city where Elizabeth wanted to get her MBA. Mark arranged a transfer to that city in order to accommodate Elizabeth's plans but felt the move was good for his career as well, as it permitted him to get more field experience.

Elizabeth and Mark initially patterned their lives together according to unconventional rules. Mark was content to work a standard workweek of forty hours and was supportive of

Elizabeth's extremely ambitious career aspirations. They had always thought that Mark would be the primary caretaker for their children, and Elizabeth would be the partner with the heavy career commitment. Mark described the situation as follows:

> For a long time we pictured ourselves in the role that Elizabeth is going to this hot business school, she's got an MBA, it's important for her to have a lot of job success. And I thought that was fine. She was making more money than me, and I liked the role of "OK, I'll do more stuff around the house, and you can go do crazy hours at work."

After Elizabeth graduated and began working, Mark started thinking about going to law school, "since all I ever did was work with attorneys anyway." Initially Mark saw law school as something to open new possibilities or give him some flexibility. He felt that he was at a "stagnant point" in his career and needed something to help him go further in his organization or in other public service jobs. Elizabeth was very supportive of this idea.

For four years Mark maintained his job full-time while going to school at night. He enjoyed a great deal of success, which opened up opportunities to him that he had not really expected when he entered law school. He had expected to return to the public or nonprofit sector upon graduation, but midway through the process he started eyeing jobs in large private law firms. While he characterized his first year in law school as one in which he was motivated by fear of failing, his attitude changed after he found out that he could potentially place at or near the top of his class. Able to see the top (and thinking that being at the top would "open up a lot more opportunities"), he started to work to achieve it. In the second year, he started engaging in such extracurricular activities as moot court and trying out for law review. His efforts paid off, and after graduation he was hired by a large law firm. At the time of being interviewed, he was in his third year of the partnership track (expected to take about nine years) and worked seven days a week, often till 10:00 P.M. each night.

This was the situation that faced Elizabeth as she approached her return to work. In some ways, it seemed a good context in which to negotiate a flexible work schedule. The organization was one committed to workplace diversity; several women had arranged part-time work schedules with their managers. Elizabeth had an excellent track record, with several letters of commendation in her personnel file from satisfied clients. She was negotiating with two women who had each recently given birth to their first child, and who were sympathetic to the emotional and scheduling strains infants could introduce to the work-family equation. And she had a husband who completely supported her in her professional decisions.

The arrangement did not, however, come to fruition. While Susan and Carol were able to identify a piece of work they estimated would take approximately twenty-four hours per week, negotiations over the more subtle terms of the working relationship broke down. Elizabeth ended up resigning from the company, and Susan hired a new person to do the work she had hoped Elizabeth would do.

What Elizabeth tried to negotiate was a discrete piece of work for which she would assume full responsibility, but which would allow her the time she wanted to be with her child. The specific job identified by Susan and Carol seemed to fit the bill. But the attempt to negotiate a viable arrangement failed because Elizabeth was unwilling to subscribe to the belief that her work involved not simply responsibility for the defined task but also an open-ended availability to the organization whenever called upon. When she sat down with Carol and Susan to negotiate the terms of her return to a part-time job, this was the issue on which the three were unable to agree: whether Elizabeth would guarantee that job demands would take precedence over her family arrangements. All three believed that Elizabeth could limit her tasks. But they differed on whether she was entitled also to limit and bound her availability to meet all standard company demands.

As the time to return to work had drawn near, Elizabeth had begun to draw boundaries around her personal life and family responsibilities. Knowing that Mark was going to be very busy, she took steps to make sure that she would be able to provide the necessary parenting to her son. She wanted to work part-time, but she did not want the work to "get out of control" and start eroding the boundaries she felt she needed. Elizabeth did not see this as an unworkable situation. She wanted to work and to do a good job at what she did, but she did not want to commit to more than she was capable of delivering. She wanted assurances that twenty-four hours per week of excellent work were going to be enough to maintain her standing in the organization.

In the early stages of the negotiations, Carol and Susan sought a verbal commitment from Elizabeth that she would do whatever was necessary to make sure the work got done. For example, Carol asked her: "What about meetings? Will you be able to come whenever there's a meeting?" When Elizabeth asked about planning meetings for the days she was in the office, Carol said, "Well, sometimes we can, but sometimes we won't be able to; then you'll have to have your day care person be more flexible." When verbal exchanges such as these failed to convince Elizabeth's managers that she would rearrange her schedule whenever they thought it necessary, they presented her with a written document outlining the terms of her arrangement as they understood them. The letter said, in essence, that the managers had a right to increase Elizabeth's hours at any point to make sure the work got done, that she had to be "totally flexible," and that she would be expected to attend all meetings scheduled during her days off. Elizabeth refused to work under these conditions.

> You have to trust that I'm going to get the job done. It's to my benefit to get the job done well, too. I certainly would not want to do the job unless I could do it well. It's been my policy, it's the way I've always done things and the way I always intend to do things. . . . I'll do the job for you, but

I don't want a letter, a contract stating that you have the right to do whatever you want and demand whatever you want from me.

It is important to note that the impression Susan and Carol had developed about Elizabeth's shifting priorities was accurate. The problem arose because Susan and Carol interpreted the new ordering of priorities as threatening to the organization. They were no longer able to see Elizabeth as "committed to the work" in the way that employees in this organization were supposed to be committed, and without this demonstration or "proof" of commitment, they were concerned that the work would not get done.

Ultimately, their suspicions that Elizabeth was unwilling to place work before her family responsibilities were confirmed when she refused to work under the written terms they drew up. The conflict over priorities was finally brought out into the open. Elizabeth made it clear that she would not allow organizational demands to encroach on her personal life past a certain point; she would not agree to subjugate her other interests to the demands of the work. Even in this progressive and flexible working world, the violation of the norm that work should take precedence in one's life rendered a resolution of the conflict impossible. Given this fundamental difference in approach to the link between the organization and private life, there was nothing for Elizabeth to do but to leave, even though she was only a few months from having her pension vested.

Three years later, when we interviewed Susan, Carol, and Elizabeth, they all still harbored a great deal of anger and resentment over the incident. Carol commented, "It isn't the way I would have liked it to go. There was something underneath not right about it." Susan recalls feeling Elizabeth was an excellent candidate for the position, and was significantly inconvenienced when Elizabeth turned it down.

She had already done the job when I was gone. She was familiar and I didn't have to teach someone else, which took me a lot of time. So she had already done it, and I was here again and I didn't want to do it. I ended up hiring someone and . . . doing a lot of the work, but she was a perfect candidate for it.

All three commented that they were surprised they still felt so much emotion and anger around the memory.

Shortly after making the decision to leave, Elizabeth was hired to work in administration at a local university. Though the job was originally designed as a full-time position, Elizabeth was able to negotiate a flexible part-time schedule as a condition for accepting the job. An agreement was made only after she visited with and obtained approval from her manager and her peers.

I had to fight for myself. I had to really step back and think about what my priorities are and—you know, in the long run, if I take some time off from my career or if I slow down, that's OK, because what's important to me now . . . and I would not have said this when I graduated from business school . . . there's just more important things to me in life right now than my career. That's the kind of thing I'm not sure I want anyone else at [this job] to know . . . but you know, I think they know that about me. I actually think I made that pretty clear when I interviewed.

Thus Elizabeth is still ambivalent about the propriety of her new priorities, even in an employment situation in which she made them explicit. It is a feeling or set of values she continues to experience, on some level, as deviant. Her view of herself as a competent professional who produces quality work and her view of herself as a mother who values motherhood above her career are difficult to reconcile.* She still feels that her reputation with her coworkers may be tarnished if they know of the precedence she gives to her family life.

*I recently heard of a female professor and her female Ph.D. student, both of whom had small children, who had a close personal relationship but *never* discussed the issues they faced in dealing with their families while pursuing their professional work.

We see in Elizabeth's remark a conflict between her ideas about professionalism and work and her personal feelings about taking care of herself and her family. Her comment illustrates the dissonance between the prevailing ideology about professionalism—that work can and should take precedence in one's life—and the conflicting belief in the ultimate value of family and children. Elizabeth at one time enjoyed feelings about work and the role of work in her life that were congruent with organizational norms. But as she attempted to adjust her priorities, she found that her feelings about her private life created tension in the workplace, where a dominant value on family is marginalized and not easily accommodated to organizational life.

Comment

Is Elizabeth Gray a failure? Not in her eyes, though she may represent a failure to the company that lost the benefit of her competence. But her story brings up a number of issues. All three women involved in Elizabeth's work situation think of what went wrong in terms of the specific people and personalities involved; none of them sees it in terms of larger social and ideological issues. Their interpretation thus reinforces the status quo.

This reading of the situation also has personal implications. Elizabeth and Mark seem to think in terms of trade-offs between one career and the other. The idea that both could pursue a high-profile career did not seem viable once children entered the picture. But if the only margin for adjustment is one's own career, or one's spouse's, then tension becomes focused on the trade-offs. Thus one might argue that organizational policies that encourage an all-or-nothing level of commitment generate family stress because they implicitly deny the possibility that the work situation could provide a margin for adjustment. What in fact is a societal issue driven by inflexibility in career structures becomes a private issue between husband and wife in which the only possible solution is for one of them to "sacrifice."

CHAPTER 6

RETHINKING COMMITMENT AND EQUITY

E lizabeth Gray left her job because her definition of commitment did not meet the criteria expected in the company. She was committed to the *task* and sure she could deliver on it; for her managers, however, this was not sufficient. From their point of view, Elizabeth was asking too much. They were used to having their employees on call: for meetings, for input on progress, for surveillance. If their own bosses wanted information (requests for which often came at unpredictable times), they needed to be able to supply it on the spot—or so they thought. *"On demand"* characterized the prevailing culture of work.

Given this culture, the concerns of the managers are understandable. But are they rational or necessary? And how much do they interfere with the ability of organizations to enlist the full potential of employees in increasingly diverse personal circumstances? One could imagine a different scenario in Elizabeth's case that would have had a better outcome but would be more difficult psychologically, since it would require a change in accepted work practices: meetings could be scheduled in advance, and managerial requests for information could be deferred to those dates. In one oil company, for instance, the dispersal of the work force through technology was found to have unexpected benefits. The manager reported that by having to schedule meetings with his group in advance, he "had to make an agenda; had to decide on priorities. [I was] surprised, but it actually helped us." Yet the need to be available for meetings is often given as an excuse for not permitting employees to work at home or to reduce their working time on a fixed schedule.

What is evident, therefore, is that managerial definitions of commitment involve more than just good performance while at work.[1] Solid work is not sufficient; commitment to work—an abstracted notion, sanctified by tradition—must supersede other commitments. As a manager who had denied permission to an employee to work five hours a week at home remarked: "It's a whole work philosophy. She comes here, she does her work, she does a good job at it. But I know when she goes home, she divorces herself from it all." The employee did good work at the office, but when her manager had to face the realization that she "divorced" herself from work when she went home, he denied her request. Unable to supervise her behavior directly, and uncomfortable with her seemingly circumscribed commitment to the job, he did not trust her with the requested arrangement.[2]

Such a definition of commitment is *not* based on mutual respect and trust, and it is not necessarily functional. Rather, it serves as a substitute for hierarchy—a way for managers to retain operational control over the work of their employees. Moreover, by sanctifying the importance of giving top priority to work, it complicates the interweaving of public and private concerns. Control by rules and hierarchy, though overly rigid for current needs, at least protects the private sphere from the intrusion of work. Not so with "commitment," which transforms an instrumental, contractual relationship into an open-ended moral bond. High-commitment organizations co-opt for the public sphere the private feelings of full responsibility and total personal involvement.[3]

Consider the case of a highly respected manager in an organization based on high commitment. Her boss and her peers have extremely positive things to say about her technical and organizational abilities, and all seem to agree that she could "write her own ticket." After her first child was born, she returned to work full-time following three months of maternity leave. Approximately eighteen months later, she started working at home one day a week; in negotiations with her manager, she worked out an arrangement whereby she continued to carry the responsibility and receive the salary of a full-time worker. The arrangement worked well, and both were satisfied.

The arrival of this woman's second child created a new situation. She now wanted to work only three days in the office and six hours at home, for a total compensation package prorated to thirty hours per week. Same employee, same peers, same organization; the only thing that had changed was her willingness to let the work define her life. Both her manager and prospective manager expressed doubts as to her commitment. Her prospective manager put it this way:

> [She] is very competent in the area, and many of the issues are the same. She's now had her second child. I don't believe she wants to return to work. She's not saying that, but I think if she had her druthers, she'd stay home. . . . She views the world differently. Her priorities have changed. Her career is not the first thing on her mind right now. I don't question these things, but what is tough is just that balance. How do you get the interesting, challenging job without the willingness to have it be a major part of your life?

Her current manager also saw a big difference in the situations with the first and second children:

They were quite different. Nothing changed with the confidence and the competence, but the jury's still out. . . . I didn't know whether the job was doable, was one issue. These are the pieces that she and I have talked about, but we're still not 100 percent open with each other. She knows—I think she knows, at some level—[that] her commitment has shifted.

Both managers recognized this woman's talents as a professional, and both respected her values as a mother. They both felt something was going to have to give, however, that she was going to have to make some tough decisions. While they could still acknowledge her skills and competence, they were finding it more difficult to continue to consider her a "professional" employee. Her level of commitment did not seem to live up to the standards of professionalism. Perhaps the most revealing remark was made by her boss, when asked if he would still rate her as a top 10 percent performer, as he had done before:

Depending on the forced ranking criteria I was using. If I were doing one as far as somebody of capability, yes. Intellect, ability to do a number of jobs, yes. If I were forced to say okay, the lifeboat exercise—if I'm going to keep one person with me—well, you need a real high energy, high commitment, high skill, high diversity of skill, and very flexible person, if you're going to have one person, she may not make the cut. . . . But she could change that, if she wanted to. It's within her control.

[Q: By driving her hours back up?]

Subjugate her other objectives.

[Q: To the work?]

Right.[4]

108

But flexible arrangements and other organizational responses to employees' family needs do not necessarily undermine an employee's commitment to organization goals. A study by the National Council of Jewish Women, for example, has shown that when employers are accommodating and flexible in their policies, pregnant women take fewer sick days, work later in their pregnancies, are *more* likely to spend time doing things related to their jobs outside regular work hours without compensation, and are more likely to return to their jobs after childbirth.[5] Further, the home-based systems developers mentioned earlier showed greater company loyalty than did their office-based counterparts: they were more likely to expect to be with the company five years later, and less likely to want to leave and set up their own private firms. These employees actually became more committed in response to the flexibility they were allowed.

In the case of Elizabeth Gray an experiment could have been set up, for a specified period of time, to test the theory that the task would get done without interfering with the rest of the work of her group. Such a scenario would have to have been based on a belief in Elizabeth's responsibility and competence, and a desire to help create the situation to make her succeed—in other words, mutual trust and respect among all the people involved. For Elizabeth's managers, it would have meant reversing the usual stance of controlling a subordinate, instead protecting her from unreasonable demands and educating their own boss to a new way of working. I suggest, based in part on the data above, that under these circumstances Elizabeth would *not* have thought only of herself, but would have made sure that she did what was needed to perform at her usual high level of work. In other words, her commitment would have emerged as a *response* to the accommodation to her private needs, not as a precondition for that accommodation.[6]

Thinking about commitment in this way is not common. For example, a 1989 book that outlines managerial strategies for obtaining superior performance identifies commitment as the key, and recommends its assessment in the following way:

Commitment, like motivation, is not something that we can observe directly. We infer that they exist because of what people say and do. There are at least two kinds of behavior that signal employee commitment. First, committed employees *appear* to be very single-minded or focused in doing their work. The second characteristic that we associate with committed employees is their willingness to make personal sacrifices to reach their team's or organization's goals.[7]

Thus commitment is gauged by a willingness to give priority to work demands, or at least to appear to do so. And how can one tell whether such willingness exists? Primarily by extended work time and unquestioned yielding to organizational demands.

Because time at work necessarily implies time away from other activities, employees who are observed to be present at the workplace for extended hours appear to be relatively more committed than their counterparts who arrive and depart at standard times. As already indicated, it is not clear that such employees actually accomplish more. It is certainly possible that they are simply less efficient at work and require more time to get the same amount of work done, or that they may create work to appear busy when in fact there is very little value added to the organization from these extra hours. Face time as an indicator of commitment, though clearly an imperfect rule, works because it unambiguously indicates that the work of the organization can and does take precedence over other aspects of one's life.[8] But in the end, it is the underlying sense of responsibility for the work that really matters.[9]

Commitment defined as the unquestioned yielding to organizational demands is curiously contradictory to current trends in organizations. Much of the writing on what has come to be called *organizational learning* throws doubt on the value of unquestioned adherence to all presumed requirements of work.[10] Such "loyalty" may actually undermine innovation and flexible adaptation to changing circumstances. In contrast, the questioning and reconsideration of demands, practices, and assumptions is necessary for organizations to learn and to make them more competitive. I would add that such rethinking may, at the same time, allow concern for employees' private lives and business goals to come together.

Proponents of the high-commitment organization base their argument on the importance of trust, participation, and shared vision to help companies become more flexible, more adaptable, and more competitive.[11] The commitment so engendered is meant to substitute for bureaucratic, hierarchical control as the way to coordinate a company's activities. But as we saw in the story of Elizabeth Gray, there are underlying cultural assumptions that may work against this goal. Elizabeth's managers felt they needed prior proof that work would be her top priority before they could agree to the new arrangement. This belief that commitment must be professed as a precondition for productive work created the problem for Elizabeth. A contrary point of view would have assumed that she would continue to be responsible about her work and allowed her, as much as possible, to define the conditions she needed to do so. Instead her managers asked her to profess and prove her commitment by agreeing in advance to meet, without question, their demands for her presence.

If commitment is really to be based on trust and respect, then it must be interpreted differently, as the thoughtful (not preprogrammed) response to organizational need. The goal would then be to establish the conditions of work in such a way as to allow employees, whatever their personal circumstances, to function in this manner as fully as possible.

Besides creating pressures on the energy and time of employees, a high-commitment, participative organization also presumes a shift in the managerial role from boss to facilitator, a shift often contradicted by accepted practices. In particular, such a new role creates questions about traditional compensation systems for managers. For example, how can managers relinquish control over the work of their subordinates if their own compensation is tied to the results of that work? And if a manager is not to be a boss who makes the decisions that others have to implement, and if the employee picks up a number of these responsibilities, then is the current discrepancy in compensation between manager and nonmanager equitable?

These are the kinds of questions that arise when commitment is analyzed critically. We want commitment because we want employees to take responsibility for their tasks, and to perform them reliably at a high level of quality. It is these end points that are important. Companies judge subcontractors and suppliers by these criteria, and they do not worry about commitment in those cases. But when it comes to in-house employees, the emphasis changes. Then commitment, instead of being seen as a means to these ends or as a by-product of appropriate work practices, is transformed into an end in itself.

Here lies the crux of the problem. The meaning of commitment as currently enacted in organizational practice transcends responsibility for the successful completion of tasks. Its demands therefore reinforce the traditional assumption underlying professional occupational roles that work takes precedence over all other aspects of life. Ironically, this assumption may actually undermine the work goals it is meant to further. So, for example, in a group of technically trained men there was a negative correlation between work involvement and family accommodation, as traditionally expected. But despite this overall trend, there was a small minority who were both involved with work and highly accommodative to family needs. Interestingly, these men exhibited technical *and* social capabilities in their work—and hence presumably were particularly valuable employees, as well as participating significantly in the everyday lives of their families.[12]

The traditional way that commitment is viewed fits a society that values activities in the public economic sphere more highly than those in the private domestic arena. In such a context, demands of high-commitment organizations increase the family-work stress of employees (see Figure 6–1). Though logically applicable to both men and women, current practice puts the onus of this pressure on women. Thus, unless women retreat back to the domestic sphere—which contradicts other current

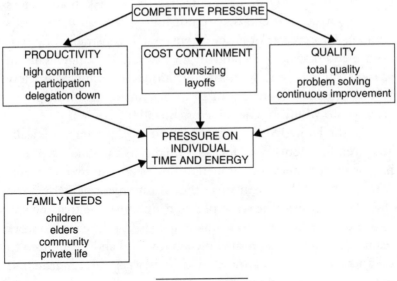

Figure 6-1

trends in American society—such pressure creates a serious equity dilemma.

EQUITY

American companies try to treat their employees equitably. For various legal, historical, and cultural reasons, this desire usually translates into an attempt to treat all employees the same (at least all in a given organizational position). But equity is not the same as uniformity. In a society as diverse as ours, where people have a great variety of needs, interests, and values, equal treatment may have unequal consequences.[13] Given such diversity, how should one think of equity?

Ideally, equity implies justice and fairness for all. One thinks of equity as the ability of people to choose how they want to live their lives in a manner dependent only on differences in temperament, interests, and skills. Whatever constraints may exist on choice would, in such an equitable world, be equivalent for all. Such a conception of equity acknowledges the fact that no one can have everything he or she desires and values, that choices must be made. But choices are not fully within an individual's control. To a greater or lesser extent, one is constrained by economic and social forces and by institutional arrangements in schools, families, and work organizations. An equitable society would equalize the impact of all these constraints on its populace; so too would an equitable organization.

In the United States, rewards in the workplace theoretically are given for merit.[14] Pay for performance is the guiding principle for most systems of compensation. There are two problems with this principle; one involves the measurement of merit,[15] and the other concerns the sense of equity and purpose that the system engenders in those to whom it applies. A self-managed work team, for example, is presumably empowered and committed to organizational goals. How should its workers be rewarded? If individual merit could be measured (and most organizations assume that it can), members of the team could get differential rewards according to their individual contribution to team performance. But such a system encourages competition among team members, which is likely to get in the way of sharing information and other necessities of coordinated work. It also is likely to demotivate most of the people at the expense of rewarding the few top performers who probably are already well motivated.

An alternative system, being tried now by a number of organizations in their effort to establish self-managed work teams, is to pay everyone on the basis of team performance. One would assume that this is a more equitable scheme, but one that top performers are likely to consider unfair. What is needed, rather, is a form of compensation that is seen as fair and yet is able to differentiate among employees of different contributions to overall performance.

An ingenious system developed at the Institute for Work Democracy would seem to meet these criteria.[16] It is based on John Rawls's theory of justice, which argues that any deviation from equality of rewards should benefit the least advantaged.[17] The institute's scheme is based on pay for performance, but a percentage of the earnings of the top performers is passed on to the other members of the team; thus everyone is motivated to improve the working of the team. Experiments have shown that this system, compared to other systems of compensation (particularly to straight pay for performance), leads to the highest productivity and the greatest sense of shared purpose and fairness.

The second problematic issue with pay-for-performance schemes is simply the measurement of merit. As we have seen, too often performance is gauged not by the quality of the output but by presumed requirements of input. Long hours and expressed willingness to put work above all other life concerns are examples of such assumed requirements. But if different groups are subject to unequal external, personal constraints on their ability to accede to such demands, inequity will necessarily result. It is clear that the fairness of rewards based on a willingness to meet organizational demands breaks down under conditions of such unequal constraints emanating from the private part of people's lives.[18] Further, given this difficulty of assessing an individual employee's contribution to the work, the tendency exists to use tangential indicators of fit. The reasoning goes as follows: if people fit the characteristics of those who have previously been successful, they are seen as more likely to be good producers than are those who are different and hence untested.[19]

Both of these difficulties with the objective assessment of performance would seem to favor the position of men in the workplace. Given the preponderance of men currently in successful positions, their characteristics are much more likely to set the terms of "fitness" than are those of women. And under current conditions, women are considerably more likely to face constraints imposed by their private lives.

Gender Equity[20]

Most work on gender equity in the workplace has centered on the question of salary (whether men and women in similar occupational roles are paid equally and whether comparable jobs, though held predominantly by one or the other sex, are equally compensated) and of status (for instance, issues of the "glass ceiling"[21]). These are manifestly critical issues. My concern, however, is with the more subtle differences in constraints that lead to inequitable treatment of women and men.

Let me start with a true story from a large manufacturing company. Sue Little is a program manager, reporting directly to the vice president of a large division of the company. She is married and has small children. Her husband brings the children to school, and Sue usually picks them up at after-school day care. Her manager thinks highly of her and completely understands her situation. One day she was at a meeting (scheduled to end at 5:00 P.M.) with the senior program manager of the division and Tim Malley, one of his project managers. At 5:30 P.M., with the meeting still not finished, Sue left to pick up her children. She regretted not being able to be present for the rest of the meeting, and the next day she complained to the vice president about meetings being held at a time that everyone knew she could not attend. He was very understanding, saying, "Don't worry, we all know about your situation, and no one minds that you have to leave."

Only Tim Malley realized that such understanding was not sufficient for equity. When Sue left, he turned to the senior program manager and said, "You know, we should have stopped the meeting." Neither the senior program manager nor the vice president grasped the fact that continuing the meeting without Sue signaled that her presence was less necessary than that of others who happened not to have the constraints of having to be at a day care center at a certain time and therefore could stay beyond the scheduled time. It was Tim's great insight to realize that real equity could only be served by stopping the meeting.

The inability to respond to differences in external constraints, or even to understand that they exist, is a prime source of inequity. I am reminded of the early 1960s and the first director of an institution geared to bringing professionally trained women back into the workplace after they took time off to bear children. The director was single and set meetings over dinner—a pleasant occasion and a nice thought, but totally disruptive for the lives of this specific group of people. In this case it was clear the arrangement would have to be changed, and it quickly was. But when the group of people with the constraints forms a minority, the inequities are harder to spot and the practices more difficult to change.

Even the more obvious concerns for equal or comparable pay and equal status run into practices that make it unlikely that there will be gender equity in the workplace. Determining salary equity depends on being able to value work and to identify the same or comparable jobs accurately. This is often difficult. Systems designed to award points to various aspects of a job in order to determine its value tend to enshrine in objective measurement differences we think are real (such as the number of subordinates) but that are only *presumed* to contribute to the actual value of a job. Such systems are based on the assumption that jobs can be defined without regard to the persons filling them. But work is not independent of the people involved, or of the specific and constantly changing situations in which it takes place. Indeed, in most adaptive organizations, jobs are defined by the people in them, not by the organization chart. As one manager in such an organization said: "This job is now 'me.' Right? It's not a job by itself. It would completely change with somebody else in it. . . . While I've got a job description right here for [a particular job], what I don't know yet is how to get this job, this work done. It will be defined by the person in the job."

The fact that jobs are defined by the jobholder is in part a characteristic of professional work generally. "In a professional's position you create most of your own work. It's not so much you're given a list of tasks. You 'gin' it up yourself. You create the work."[22] And even in more traditional and more formal organizations, "idiosyncratic jobs"—those not specified in the abstract but created for and by particular people—can play an important role in the organization's work.[23] The problem for equity is that if salary is linked to a carefully predefined job with an objectively attainable value, it is likely to perpetuate existing conditions that often entail subtle sources of inequitable rewards.

Attaining status equity is also not easy. It is complicated by the dubious presumption that high-level employees are continuously oriented to moving up within an organizational hierarchy. Particularly for people trying to integrate their public and private lives, occupational status is usually not the whole story; a way of life that includes autonomy and control of their time can be more valuable than money and power. For example, one investigator meeting with a group of high-level women in a large, progressive company was surprised to hear that the latter no longer wanted to move up because of the life-style that higher positions imposed. And it turned out that some men in the same company were thinking along the same lines, though much more hesitatingly.[24]

What employers do not know, of course, is the context in which such "choices" are made—particularly the demands and expectations coming from outside the employing organization, from families or from society at large.[25] And it is here that the deeper sources of inequity often reside. Individual choice based on differences in external constraints will not lead to equity if organizational procedures presume that such demands are irrelevant.

What creates the problem of gender equity, therefore, is that constraints are not equivalent. Women are subject to many more family constraints, which leads some analysts to conclude that gender equity in the workplace will not be possible without gender equity in the family.[26] This may be true, but the more immediate problem is the overall lack of recognition and legitimation by American companies of family needs for men as well as women. In fact, it is often more difficult for a man to arrange a flexible work schedule than it is for a woman. When asked if he would entertain the request by a father to work at home one day per week, one manager said he would use the same criteria as for a woman, but that "it would feel a little funny." His thinking went along the following lines:

[What is the] motivation driving this person to want to do it? If he just wants to be at home because he likes to fly model airplanes, or embroider, I probably would be less inclined to make it happen. But for somebody who is clearly

118

an aggressive, high need–achievement oriented person, who needs to be a great parent and a great employee, I'd be willing to say yes. But if I've got somebody who says well, I just want to goof off, take my time . . . so just cut my hours so I can do something else that I'd rather do. . . . [Then] I would not be as inclined to do it.[27]

In the story of Sue Little, only Tim Malley understood these equity issues. His intervention, however, indicates that it was not really necessary to carry on that meeting at just that time (or he would not have made the suggestion). But the surprise with which his comment was met shows the difficulty of absorbing into organizational practice the understanding of the impact of differential constraints. It is not sufficient to tolerate them or even to understand them, as the vice president and senior program manager did. Rather, what is needed is a reevaluation of the practices that make such understanding necessary to begin with. Only then will constraints not have a differential impact on women and men; only then can we begin to approach gender equity in the workplace.

So the principles of equity can be stated, though their enactment in organizational life is clearly difficult. But a number of questions remain. Why should organizations be concerned with this issue? Why should they not continue their current way of judging "merit"—even if it means that many more men than women are likely to move to high positions? Is there a reason to believe that a more equitable practice would benefit the organization? We will see some examples of possible benefits in the final chapters. Suffice it to mention here that present practice also leads to burnout and midlife crises; it also encourages individual competition at a time when coordinated and empowered teams are seen as more likely to help America's competitive position.

CONCLUDING NOTE

Conditions for equal salary and equal status are not the same as those for equal life satisfaction (defined as a satisfactory balance between public and private lives). Individual choice must find a route among these seemingly contradictory paths. But such choice will only be equitable if the constraints on choice—from work organizations, from family, and from societal expectations—are equivalent for men and women. Men need to feel as free to take parental leave and to opt for flexible arrangements as women. This means that organizations must accept the fact that their employees cannot give exclusive commitment to their work, and they must grant equal legitimacy to the multiple commitments of their male and female employees—something they already do for illness. But this in turn implies a dramatic rethinking of the structure of the work place and the procedures that justify and reinforce it. It also implies real trust in the sense of responsibility with which employees deal with the demands upon them.

CHAPTER 7

PATHWAYS TO CHANGE

T raditional career rules favor employees who put work above everything else. Their time and commitment belong to the company; private needs are assumed not to exist and are accommodated only on an ad hoc, exceptional basis. "Organizational transformation,"[1] geared to creating a more competitive position for American business, proceeds without thought for people's personal concerns. Family benefits, if they exist at all, are entirely separate from policies aimed at improving productivity, and the result often is contradictory pressures on employees. The stories of Elizabeth Gray and Nancy Wright—though they reacted in very different ways—portray the individual and organizational costs of these existing practices.

The separation of concern with productivity from consideration of family benefits reflects the cultural divide between the public and private spheres. As we have seen, this creates a situation where either the needs of the private domain are neglected or the population divides according to primary responsibility for one or the other sphere. Given the economic and psychological position of women, it is they who must concentrate on caretaking under this second alternative. And when they do so, given current career rules, they are forced to retreat from the core positions in organizational life that they have slowly been approaching and for which companies have been trying to prepare them.

This is the basic dilemma that current conditions present. The key question is whether one can devise organizational processes that deal simultaneously with productivity and with family or other personal concerns, and that do not depend for their success on highly differentiated gender roles. To solve this problem is not an easy task, as examples from other countries make evident. The Japanese, for instance, are expert at organizing work for productivity—indeed, our current view of productive organizational forms is a reflection of their efforts. But they deal with the caretaking issue by sacrificing gender equity altogether. Sweden is often seen as a model on social issues, but the situation there also illuminates the difficulties. The Swedes are very good in supporting the family by means of an elaborate government/business infrastructure supported by higher taxes. But even they have not been able to create a workplace where women and men participate equally.

Nowhere have the assumptions about the required conditions of work and the accepted manner of defining and achieving career success been basically altered; nowhere has the traditional mold been broken. The public occupational world remains independently valued and separate from the vital concerns of domestic life, a differentiation buttressed by the pervasive gender structuring of roles. Two cultural divides—between the economic and domestic spheres and between male and female—define people's position within the work-family system (see Figure 4–1).

An equitable resolution of the present problems depends on a blurring of the distinctions in both of these divides, which should be possible since the divisions are cultural, not biological. Such a change would reduce gender distinctions by seeing them as individual differences, and it would weaken the association of influence and power with the occupational realm. In an ideal form, the work required in the two spheres would be seen as equally legitimate and equally valued, and as contributing equally to both the society and the individual's sense of identity. But to say that change along these lines is possible is not to say that it is easy; it would require fundamental alterations in social values and organizational practice.

When employees themselves are asked what they would require from organizations in order to resolve this dilemma, their responses are fairly limited. Elizabeth Gray feels that her boss, Carol, should have been able to buffer her from some of the organizational demands that seemed to make her situation untenable:

> Had Carol been willing to say to these managers, "Elizabeth is working part-time so you just have to take that into account; we'll make sure your work gets done for you, and it won't be a problem"—had Carol been willing to do that, I don't think it would have been an issue for any of those people.

And Martha Chase wishes that organizations would provide leave to care for sick children and permit flexible working hours whenever possible. Fundamental change, she feels, depends on government and on society at large, not on work organizations:

> I've thought about some policies that would be effective. More generally, just public policy awareness about raising children. We're entering another baby boom, and the political and social agenda should be more receptive to children. That would translate into concrete policies, like higher deductions for dependents, better schools, more aggressive

policies about airing questionable TV programs when children are awake. It's extra hard today to raise children when there's so much about drugs and other subjects inappropriate for children. Schools aren't so good, leaving a burden on parents. . . . [Private corporations] could support things to improve schools that would improve their labor force.

None of these suggestions would fully resolve the basic dilemma. Though they would make life easier for caretakers of children, they would not protect the careers of those who took advantage of them. Any real resolution requires a new approach not only to children but to work, and that is absent in these suggestions.

One aspect of such a new approach to work was commented on by Matthew Langley, a graduate of a major business school, when he reflected on his career ten years after his MBA. The experience of working for a small consulting firm stands out in his mind. He greatly admired "the approach of the guy [the boss]":

He would say, "Dress if you're going to meet a client—otherwise it doesn't matter." His policy was "no suits if no client effect." If you don't need to come in, fine. There was flexibility; trusting you to know made a tremendous difference. And so we worked harder, with freedom—nothing getting in the way [of work]—it makes so much sense.

In that situation, flexibility and discretion were not directed specifically to family needs but were part of the accepted way of doing work. Matthew is now thinking of creating his own company, where he says he would know how to treat people and get the work done:

I would not beat heads, but give responsibility and opportunity. . . . I would create an environment that would reflect me—where I could take my shoes off, where people could work anywhere, forty hours a week only if necessary. Only performance would count. . . . People have different balances and could spend a day at home if they had the

skills and ability and the discipline to do what is required . . . [one] would need to bring trust—to trust one's
intuition and one's insight.[2]

OLD AND NEW ASSUMPTIONS

To think clearly about the difference between the traditional mode based on control and this more trusting way of responding to employee needs, it helps to start by outlining old,
constraining assumptions and juxtaposing new ones that help
employees reconcile the needs of work and family (see Figure
7–1.)[3] In the current system, as detailed in the previous chapter,
continuous and total commitment is presumed to be necessary
for the successful performance of organizational tasks. Further,
putting work above all else is most critical in the early career
years, for as Rosenbaum has shown, promotions not achieved
during this period seldom occur at a later date.[4] But these early
years are also the ones in which there are the greatest demands
from a growing family. Where once this dilemma was resolved by
men attending to the needs of career and leaving the needs of
family to their wives, the current increase in dual careers necessitates other accommodations.

To defer having children or not to have them at all is one
possible solution; to buy infant care, sick child care, toddler day

OLD ASSUMPTIONS (constraining)	NEW ASSUMPTIONS (facilitating)
CONTINUOUS COMMITMENT	DISCONTINUITY
MANAGE VIA INPUT (based on control)	ACCOUNTABILITY FOR RESULTS (based on trust)
HOMOGENEITY (in outlook and values)	LEARNING FROM DIVERSITY (self-design)

Figure 7–1

Adapted from D.H. Montross and C.J. Shinkman (eds.), *Career Development in the 1990s: Theory and Practice* (1992). Courtesy of Charles C Thomas, Publisher, Springfield, Illinois.

care, and after-school care—if these exist and are affordable—is another. What is not possible, under current assumptions, is to defer the total involvement with career. Yet there is hardly any convincing evidence to indicate that the premium placed on work in these early years is particularly productive over the long run. On the contrary, we are beset with burnout, plateaus, and midlife crises. These organizational maladies tend to be seen as weaknesses of individuals, and efforts are made to "clear out the deadwood." What is ignored is the way the traditional structure of careers contributes to these outcomes. Individual midcareer difficulties are embedded in the pressures of the early career, and in the assumption that a career is a continuous upward movement in an organizational hierarchy.[5]

Since the presumption of continuity also creates difficulties later for the organization, an assumption of discontinuity is more effective in the long run. This means dividing the career into independent segments, each with its own distinctive distribution of involvement between the public and the private spheres. Segments of work with low involvement would be judged differently from those with high involvement, and they would involve a different portfolio of tasks with different levels of reward. A period of some withdrawal from work would not be considered evidence of failure or of an inability to be productive, blemishes that would stay with the employee for the rest of his or her career.

Nor would periods of low involvement reduce the effectiveness of organizations. There is always work that is less visible, more circumscribed, and perhaps less complex that can be allocated to workers in that phase. What is critical is that evaluation—and rewards—would not be the same for these tasks as for those requiring greater employee investment of time and energy. Under these conditions, the evidence indicates that workers would show high levels of commitment and responsibility for the tasks they are assigned.

A second assumption concerns the role of management in the system of authority. The constraining assumption, based on principles of hierarchy, is that managers must personally control every decision, thus creating elaborate systems of before-the-fact approval. In one oil company, for example, field representatives were not allowed to make pricing decisions for the gasoline stations in their area without going up the line to gain approval.[6] Expertise and the necessary information were assumed to reside at the top; hence managers monitored not only results but the way decisions were made.

There are fundamental difficulties, however, with this assumption. Local information is characteristically more available to the working-level employee (the field representative, in this case) and is probably more critical for the pricing decision than is general expertise. Further, computer technology makes it possible for working-level employees to obtain any general information they may need. In fact, this oil company was slowly moving toward accountability at a lower level, with management monitoring not the process but the results of decision making. Such a change from continuous surveillance to after-the-fact review must be based on principles of trust. It has a number of potentially valuable consequences: it creates more commitment on the part of the working-level employees and simultaneously permits more discretion over the way they spend their time, which in turn allows them to have greater control over their lives.

Finally, there is the assumption that homogeneity in values and outlook is beneficial. Employees are selected to fit a dominant mode or are socialized in that direction; "misfits" are weeded out if all else fails. Such procedures, however, can lead to routinization and to lack of innovation and creativity.[7] In contrast, the view that innovative organizations require experimentation drawn from a large repertoire of possible responses—the assumption underlying self-design[8]—is better served by diversity.

Learning from Diversity

Diversity in the U.S. work force looms as a key issue for organizations in the coming years, and as a result many companies are introducing training on how to manage diversity and value differences.[9] But the critical point that diversity can be a source of organizational learning is often missed. Far from simply being a problem that needs to be managed, diversity provides the opportunity for an organization to learn about itself and to devise new procedures in line with changing conditions.

In one company, for example, a Malaysian employee who was not promoted to a managerial position as quickly as an American in his group complained that his manager had discriminated against him.[10] The manager reported that the employee was doing very well at his job, and had never indicated that he *wanted* a promotion. But the Malaysian had felt that asking for a promotion was pushy and inappropriate—and so he was overlooked. He might have made an excellent manager, however, which raises a number of questions: Was the company missing out on good people? Is pushing oneself forward a necessary requirement for being a manager, particularly in an age when teamwork is highly valued? The complaint of the Malaysian might have led the company to ask such questions and to realize that expecting people to demand advancement might be depriving it of those who would manage in a different way, perhaps more appropriately for current needs. Diversity might have been a source of organizational learning.

Or take the example of the Xerox Corporation, which has been extremely proactive in dealing with minority groups. At one point, when it was shown that black salespeople were being assigned to smaller, more chancy, and less lucrative sales districts, Xerox changed its principles of assignment.[11] But it did not go the whole distance by questioning whether the way it compensated its sales force reflected the actual conditions and requirements of different districts. Had it done so, it might have devised a new form of compensation that would have benefited all employees, not only those who initially were found to be disadvantaged by the old system.

Learning from diversity requires one to confront, develop, and profit by differences, not merely to tolerate them. Organizations can use the fact that different people perceive things differently, respond differently to procedures, behave in different ways, and have different needs to question the way things have always been done and to explore the possibilities of improving organizational processes. But to do so requires linking diversity to general organizational issues; it cannot be treated only as an individual problem that needs to be micromanaged. Insofar as organizations fail to see social and cultural differences among their employees as a source of new ideas and an opportunity to reconsider traditional practice, diversity does not play a constructive role, and learning from changing circumstances in the work force is not built into normal procedures.[12]

Thus, the old constraining assumptions of continuous commitment, management via input, and homogeneity (listed on the left side of Figure 7–1) need to be changed. They need to be replaced by discontinuity, accountability for results, and learning from diversity (listed on the right side of Figure 7–1). It is interesting to note that organizations that follow the precepts of "high commitment" are moving toward the bottom two assumptions of the more facilitative side of Figure 7–1. In theory at least, high-commitment systems are based more on trust than control,[13] and the assumption of homogeneity is necessarily relinquished because of the influx of new groups of people. Hence diversity is assumed in these organizations, though few if any view their diverse work force as an opportunity for learning. But the belief in continuous commitment persists and is even being strengthened. *Discontinuity* therefore is a key element in the idealized, facilitative system represented by the right side of Figure 7–1. To devise a career system that does not jeopardize gender equity and still meets both the requirements of productivity and the needs stemming from personal concerns rests critically on procedures that permit discontinuity.

Despite beliefs to the contrary, evidence of the advantages of career discontinuity is available. Studies of second careers (embarked on after midlife career changes) show the benefits of change and the costs associated with pressures of the early years in the traditional career.[14] The same studies show that tasks associated with the early parts of a career can be successfully tackled by middle-aged people. It is possible to get professional training and start a second career even as a lawyer or architect; it is certainly possible to start a successful small business relatively late in life. Indeed, a whole class of people—those in the military—systematically incorporate second careers into their life plans.[15] And breaking the "one life–one career imperative"[16] has become increasingly important in an era of downsizing, retrenchment, and rapidly changing technology.

A study from a time when few women embarked on technical careers is also relevant.[17] It contrasts single career women with married women who at midcareer are fully involved in their jobs. The single women followed traditional, linear careers; though they all changed jobs and organizations at least once, they worked continuously and remained committed to their original career choices. These linear paths, typical of the traditional male career pattern, contrast sharply with those of the married women studied, who arrived at midcareer by a different route. All but one of the latter had a "slow" or low-involvement period in their career histories, leaving jobs because of a family move prompted by a husband's relocation. But these interruptions were not detrimental. At midlife all these women saw themselves on a rising career trajectory and anticipated greater success at work in the years ahead. None of the single women shared this optimistic view of the future.

The reactions of the married women to their careers and to their work were consistently more positive than those of the single women whose careers followed more traditional lines: the former were more involved with their work and more professionally established. This small group of married women was able to reach a midlife work situation that fitted their lives and was productive for their employers, even though they had interrupted their careers to some extent. Thus organizational careers can survive slow starts, late entrances, and midcourse changes of direction, and may even benefit from such unorthodoxies.

Such discontinuity, on a wider scale, is critically needed now. It fits a period of retrenchment and downsizing, and it may in fact not be so alien after all. As one independent consultant has remarked:

If you think of executive training programs, people are given a very general menu in the early years of their career—spending as much time in strategic planning as on the floor, say—in many different parts of the organization before moving into a traditional career track. In [this] model, that becomes the norm. If you can elongate that cycle—over the course of a career, say—you'd spend time in a variety of tasks, sometimes working in groups, sometimes by yourself, or as a department of one, constantly changing the focus of what you do, how you do it, and with whom.[18]

And this changing focus could also include times when one is more involved with family affairs than with work.

CHANGING PROCEDURES

How can one introduce discontinuity into a career system based on accountability and trust as well as on diversity? What procedures would flow from these facilitating assumptions? How would they play themselves out in the reality of organizational life? To answer these questions one has to confront the issues discussed in the previous chapters—time, autonomy, commitment, and equity—and relate them to the productivity needs of U.S. corporations.

Individuals need control over time, and they must be allowed to limit their commitment to the responsible completion of tasks. Organizations need creative adaptability from their employees and their willingness to be accountable for their actions. The changes in career procedures that would be necessary for both of these needs to be met add up to a very different system of career development than is now generally found.

Traditional career assessment is based on long-term planning for an individual's eventual position. It has linear continuity built into it; it presumes that the appropriate career direction is up, and that what happens at the beginning is a strong deter-

minant of the future. Most often effort is put into early identification of future potential with little concern for the long-range
consequences of such decisions. This procedure ignores the possibility that the selection itself may determine the outcome (by
the self-fulfilling prophecy) and assumes that it is easy to specify
the requirements of future work and to relate desired results to
particular contributions. All of this limits individuals as well as
organizations. What is needed is a system that assumes not a
continuous progression toward some predefined job, but alter-
nating times of low and high investment in work. Such a system,
which might be called *zero-based career planning*, would permit
employees to reenter the contest for influential positions without
elimination in the early rounds.[19] Such a system would depend
on individual negotiation built around discontinuous career segments, each of which could be based on a different level of involvement.

What would such individual negotiations look like?[20] They
would necessarily be bound by the period of time to which they
would apply, itself a negotiable point. The central focus of the
negotiation would be the extent of investment the individual is
willing to give to work for the specific time period under review.
Such a process requires individuals to take responsibility for
assessing their own priorities and for translating them into
practical programs. Organizations in turn have to accept these
programs as legitimate and viable and adjust the requirements of
a particular job to varying degrees of employee involvement.
Elizabeth Gray was trying, though unsuccessfully, to pursue such
a negotiation with her managers.

By definition, such a system is not based on career procedures that apply uniformly to all people. To be able to make the
differentiation necessary for such individual negotiations to
work, *disaggregation* would be necessary. Our current system
tightly couples task with position, influence, salary, and status;
this would have to change. For example, management itself
would have to be defined as a task available for a period of
time—perhaps a period of high involvement—and not as a status
to be achieved once and for all. In some cases, sophisticated

dual-career ladders allow a movement back from management without penalty. And deans—even presidents—of universities frequently go back to teaching after a certain period of time. But most business organizations that use the dual ladder have generally not dealt with this issue very successfully.[21]

Disaggregation of tasks from position and pay is necessary if work and compensation are to be attached to people, not to disembodied jobs. It permits more flexibility in the deployment of human resources and encourages the greater adaptability and creativity needed by today's organizations.[22] Some disaggregation has already occurred. IBM no longer has a maximum salary for its engineering positions, thus allowing engineers to increase their compensation without having to shift to nonengineering tasks. And skills-based pay, which is becoming more prevalent in production work, begins to address the same issue. Much more, though, is needed.

Control over time, individual negotiation, and disaggregation represent the keys to a career system that combines discontinuity with accountability and diversity. Ideally it allows organizations to meet their productivity needs and employees to meet their personal needs. Such a system requires companies to rethink career paths and procedures, and to reevaluate the organization of work and the practices and reward systems that buttress it. It will not be sufficient to deal with employees' personal issues simply as add-ons to a system designed only to increase productivity.

PROBLEMS

Change is always difficult, and a new system's problems are particularly evident. Some problems only surface with use, but some can be anticipated. I deal here with three concerns that can most readily be raised about the suggestions presented in this chapter.

Problem 1: It is individual negotiation that accounted for discrimination against women and minorities and resulted in efforts to make procedures uniform so that they would be equal and fair to all.

This is true. As already indicated, though, uniformity is not necessarily fair or equitable. The only answer to this problem is to be actively aware of the possibility that individual negotiation may be based on stereotyped expectations about groups of people. In the family area, it means making sure that men and women can take equal advantage of such family benefits as flexible schedules and parental leave. It will require careful monitoring as well as commitment and modeling by senior management to ensure that real equity exists in a system based on individual negotiation.

Problem 2: But there are people who like to work long hours and like to give their sole priority to work. They will have to be rewarded, and they will therefore always move ahead faster than those who have periods of lesser involvement—or if they do not, they will feel that they should.

Three points need to be made about this. First, under a system of true discontinuity, employees in a low-involvement phase will not expect to move ahead as fast as those with high occupational investment. They will assume that their movement will occur when they shift to high involvement, and will not have been jeopardized by the slower period. Nor will movement always be up or be dependent on a predefined series of steps. Second, there are both intrinsic and extrinsic rewards to work. The person who wants to put in longer hours than actually required by the work to be done should be doing it for intrinsic reasons, and should not expect also an increase in extrinsic rewards; let the pleasure of the work and the working situation carry the rewards for this input. This would ensure that it is *only* intrinsic pleasure that motivates such an excessive input of time to work. Third, in this ideal system the work—reorganized to be optimally efficient—would be spread over enough people so that individual needs concerning time could be met.

Problem 3:   If family and other personal needs are accepted as legitimate reasons for declining assignments that involve travel and long hours of work, then the employee without such an excuse will be unfairly expected to accept such assignments.

Two considerations apply here. First, the legitimacy of declining an assignment for personal reasons, without fear of long-range career consequences, needs to apply to *all* employees, not only to those whose family situation (as seen from the outside) seems to warrant it. Second, if an unwelcome assignment is accepted, it should be rewarded; but the reward should be specific to the particular assignment. It therefore should not consist of an increase to salary or figure in a promotion. A bonus or, if desired, a period of free time would be more appropriate.

Problems such as these are not trivial, but neither are they insurmountable. And if they are seen as opportunities for rethinking current procedures, their explicit acknowledgment can in itself further the process of change.

As an example of how private concerns can be explicitly linked with the arrangements of work, let us deal with the need of employees to have more private time. At the moment, companies work on the following stylized assumption:

Everyone knows that top performers spend most of their time working. They certainly don't leave their offices at 5 o'clock.

This is a problem, of course, if one has to pick up a child at 5:30. The company's typical response is either to provide after-hours day care spots (for which the employee is grateful, but which may have unacknowledged repercussions for families) or, more likely, to create an implicit—if not explicit—secondary track for employees who do not fit the traditional criteria for top performance. Such a path is almost always a "mommy track" and therefore works against women and against the goal of gender equity.

But instead of thinking of the family need as a secondary

object of concern, let us turn the issue around and *start* with it. In the present example, let us consider 5:00 P.M. the top limit of the workday, a preexisting constraint on which no negotiation is possible. Everyone leaves, including the boss; the door is locked. Such an approach changes the response to work-family issues dramatically. The question now is not what can be done to make it easier for people to stay past 5:00 but how to get the work done by then. Such a change forces one to rethink from scratch the way to do the work. The usual approach, which considers only how to make it possible for employees to stay late, does not require one to do this; it assumes that one is doing the work in the best (and perhaps the only) way possible.

As already mentioned, such a process actually happened in a software company.[23] The employees of that company stopped the drift to longer days by rethinking the way they had been proceeding. Instead of picking up assignments at random, they now began planning at the start: checking the whole pile of work, figuring out the best order in which to do it, and determining the best people to do each part. This change, plus less wasted time, is the kind of improvement that companies wish their employees would achieve in any case. It came about in this situation because it was motivated by both personal *and* work needs.

This simple example involves two distinct departures from current assumptions and procedures. First, it represents a different meaning of time. The goal here is to work smart, not long; in fact, the two are now seen as antithetical, and long hours are transformed from indicators of commitment to signs of inefficiency. More critical is the point that commitment is now an *output* of change, not a precondition. The causal order has been reversed (see Figure 7–2): commitment now emerges in response to the changed conditions of work, which are premised, in part, on employees' personal needs. The home-based systems developers described earlier, for example, showed more commitment to their work than did their office-based peers.

Such a change by definition eases the individual conflict between work and family. But what about the work? What happens, for example, when a customer calls at 5:05 P.M.? The

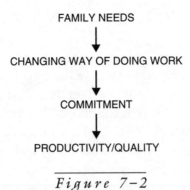

FAMILY NEEDS

↓

CHANGING WAY OF DOING WORK

↓

COMMITMENT

↓

PRODUCTIVITY/QUALITY

Figure 7-2

suggestion here is again a rethinking of presumed requirements, which might take the form of the following questions:

1. *Is it necessary for the customer to have off-hours access?* There is some indication that customers who have restricted access actually organize their own work more effectively.[24] But if off-hours access *is* necessary, proceed to the next question.

2. *How else, besides the employee staying late, could the customer be served?* Technology is a help. Customer service can now be accomplished without office presence (the service representative could be at home, or all calls after 5:00 in one time zone could be transferred to people in an earlier time zone). If technology cannot help, then train other people on a part-time basis to take the off-hours calls (perhaps students or retired employees). Such training could have other beneficial ramifications.

If no possibility exists to redefine the responses to a customer's needs, then the job may not be amenable to the time constraint.

The key point is that usually these questions are not even asked, because it is assumed that customer service must be available at all hours and must be handled by a particular person sitting in an office. But if they are asked, it is more likely than not that alternative work arrangements are possible. And such arrangements may turn out to have unexpected positive consequences.

137

CONCLUDING NOTE

These suggestions would have to be tailored to each organization; they represent a general perspective on change, not a single prescribed procedure. They are based on the idea that uniform, rigid systems no longer fit current conditions, and that career practices must reflect the particular needs of both the organization and its individual employees. Though such changes will not be easy to introduce and to manage, they are necessary if organizations are to compete in a diverse and rapidly changing world and at the same time allow their employees to deal more constructively with private concerns.

These changes represent a different view of career development based on combining the legitimacy of private needs with a rethinking of the conditions of work. They depend on a reevaluation of what is really needed to be productive in a job, along with a belief and trust in people's willingness to contribute according to their abilities and personal situations. Only by such a detailed rethinking of work and career will it be possible to integrate American companies' productivity needs with the personal issues now confronting the work force. Without it, we run the risk of greatly increasing the stress on individual employees, to the detriment of the productive commitment of today's—and tomorrow's—work force.

CHAPTER 8

ENVISIONING THE FUTURE

A s the previous chapters make clear, to deal with the challenges ahead the organizational world will have to encompass—more than it has ever done before—discontinuity and heterogeneity in careers and in work patterns. Such a world will be based on new ways of thinking about the relation between work and family and on new meanings attached to time and to commitment. It will be a world based on trust, one in which employees will be assumed to be responsible for their work without the imposition of detailed operational controls. It may also be a more equitable world than the one we now know.

In such an organizational world, attuned to the diverse needs of employees and sensitive to changes in the larger society, both individuals and society at large would benefit. More people would be able to participate in paid work, and fewer would have to subsume all other interests to the demands of employment. Such a world would allow people to link their public and private lives more easily. And there would be a less rigid gender divide; women and men could meet occupational and personal requirements in as many different ways as their diversity justified. Society would also gain by decreasing the social ills that stem from a lack of support for the care of families and communities.

Such a world, one hopes, would give all individuals more choice about how to live their lives. To be sure, as expectations for behavior become less standardized and less obviously programmed, each person would become more dependent on his or her own sense of identity, in work as in family. Such freedom to choose implies the necessity to know what one wants, which is not always an easy task. But at least it would be a world where the costs and benefits are not gender specific and can be shared more equitably.

For companies, it would mean a different, seemingly more chaotic way of dealing with their employees.[1] Individual arrangements would have to be made, and the requirements of work would have to be more carefully defined. Diversity would be an opportunity for learning rather than a problem, and it is learning (defined as examining and modifying basic assumptions in response to emerging needs) that is critical for organizational survival.[2] Though such an environment may seem difficult to manage, perhaps one can take comfort from descriptions of disorder in the new science of chaos. In the words of one early proponent in this new field, chaos may provide "liberated systems" with "exciting variety, richness of choice, a cornucopia of opportunity"[3]—a description that fits an organization able to learn.

To surface and rethink assumptions, however, is not easy. Nor is it easy to unearth practices embedded in older assumptions that now may be interfering with the solution of emerging problems. For example, engineering companies often hire many engineers at the beginning of a project, and when it ends, they are left with underutilized and demoralized employees. A possible solution is to hire more technicians to do some of the "engineering" work; and when demand declines, their skills are more easily transferred to the ensuing maintenance jobs. One company, when confronted with this "obvious" solution, resisted its implementation. It took a while to establish that the resistance stemmed from a decision made long before, under entirely different circumstances, to base managers' compensation in part on the number of engineers—not technicians—who reported to them. The problem of retaining engineering managers (the reason for the policy) had changed, but the embedded practice constrained the innovation necessary for current conditions.

It may also be necessary to question assumptions about the social world. One manager in a multinational high-tech manufacturing company had to send an employee to an Asian site shortly before Christmas, a time when the employee was expecting to bring his freshman daughter home from college for the first time. The manager handled the situation with consideration and provided a "merit" bonus that allowed the employee to fly his daughter home. Some questions might be raised about this response. According to the suggestions in the previous chapter, one might first ask whether it was really necessary to take the trip just at that time. But if it was, one might then question the assumption that this particular employee needed to visit the Asian site. After all, there is only one father to every daughter, but there should be other qualified employees who could take the trip.[4] If not, this would be vivid evidence for the need to move in the direction of more multifunctional working groups.

The rethinking of taken-for-granted procedures and underlying assumptions is critical for the new organizational world. Neither ad hoc accommodations for individual employees nor the setting of new policies at the margin will create the kind of environment that will allow employees to manage their lives better while helping the business become more productive. As many companies are learning, transforming themselves into more competitive organizations requires change at a basic, cultural level. To be effective under current conditions, such change *must* take into account—from the beginning—the personal needs of employees.

An interesting example is reported by Lois E. Kelly, president of a marketing communications firm.[5] In the company's second year of operation, during which it increased its client base and income twofold, a number of women critical to the work of Kelly's staff took maternity leaves. She described her reactions vividly: "Troubling questions raced through my head. How could we deliver the service we promised? . . . How would we meet our income forecasts? . . . How could they do this to me?" Looking back on that year, however, she realized that everything went well and that she and the organization actually gained by the experience.

> The most important lesson was learning to trust *completely* my colleagues' understanding of the situation and their ability to manage change. . . . They knew client expectations had to be met. They understood the need to cultivate the firm's good, yet young and tenuous, reputation. They wanted as much as ever to achieve our financial goals. And they did.

Each of these employees made her own plan for handling her responsibilities while on leave, and those employees who remained during these staff leaves discovered talents they never knew they had. "It is not enough to ask employees for their ideas. You must depend on those same employees to act on the ideas to solve the situation—whether the issue is maternity-leave staffing or correcting a manufacturing problem."

To legitimate people's private needs is not a call for paternalism, for employers to make decisions for employees based on their knowledge of the private situation of these employees. Rather, it represents a willingness to adapt work to a more holistic view of people and to accept their necessarily circumscribed relation to the company in which they work. The Kelly example also makes the essential point that such a stance will not hurt the productivity of the firm.

This different way of looking at the working world reflects a new understanding of boundaries between an employee and an organization, and between a person's public and private life. Current processes assume that the employee is closely tied to the demands of the employing organization, that work must come first and organizational demands must be met. Hence there is assumed to be a clear separation between the person as worker and that person in the private domain. A tight link within the boundary of the organization imposes a formidable barrier between the public and private domains. What is needed is a loosening of the link between organization and employee, and a closer linking of public and private life.

An interesting example comes from a study of fast food restaurants that compared those franchised and managed by individual owners with those wholly owned by the central company and managed by one of its employees.[6] The latter case represents the typical link between the employee and organization, whereas the former is representative of a looser link (which one also sees in a number of other subcontracting relationships).

Two results relevant to our concerns emerged from this study. The franchisee was less easy to control, as one might expect; for example, when Pizza Hut decided to include evening delivery in its services, one franchisee refused to go along with this company decision because he did not want to spend his evenings working.. This was possible for him because of the nature of the franchise contract, whereas an employee manager would not have had this option. The looser tie between employee and organization allowed this individual to manage the tie between work life and private life in a more idiosyncratic but more personally satisfactory way. The company, naturally, found such individuality problematic. But the central control of employee managers did not create a favorable context for new ideas; it turned out that most of the new and profitable ideas came from the outlets that were franchised. McDonald's "Egg McMuffin," for example, was a franchise idea. Loosening the links between the organization and the employee thus may help both sides of this relationship.

SOURCES OF RESISTANCE

Despite such examples and the evident logic behind them, organizations (particularly, perhaps, their human resource departments) are reluctant to deal with their employees in a more flexible way. They resist implementing as policy, or allowing individuals to implement as ad hoc accommodations, arrangements that help employees bridge their multiple roles.

A first source of resistance lies in a basic mistrust of the willingness and ability of employees to take responsibility for the work of the organization while also giving high priority to their private lives. Such a mistrust reflects a *disbelief in intrinsic motivation*. As McGregor noted as early as 1960,[7] a prevalent managerial view of human behavior (what he called Theory X) is that "the average human being has an inherent dislike of work and will avoid it if he can [and] prefers to be directed, wishes to avoid responsibility, [and] has relatively little ambition." Such a worker must be controlled by extrinsic means—the carrot and the stick. Intrinsic motivation, which stems from the demands of the task itself, is assumed not to exist.

Of course, social scientists have long known—and most individuals' personal experience can corroborate—that many activities are pursued for their own sake.[8] And some companies are trying to incorporate this awareness into their management practices. IBM's leadership training, for example, includes a film of children at play that vividly demonstrates the naturalness of involvement with a task: the children are engrossed in their activities, and there is no external reward. The purpose of the film is to help managers recognize that their employees have an inherent capacity and desire to do their work that is lost if circumscribed by too many rules and regulations.

A second source of resistance to individualized and flexible arrangements, and one frequently cited by personnel departments, is the *fear of precedence*. Every suggested modification of practice is seen as precipitating an avalanche of response. But actual experience denies this concern. For example, many organizations are currently faced with the issue of whether to extend medical and other benefits to the domestic partners (not only spouses) of their employees, a move that could potentially be very costly if many people were involved. Institutions that have established such benefits, however, have found a minimal burden added to the insurance system; in the city of Seattle, for example, one-third fewer people applied than were expected, and the insurers dropped the initial expectation of an added premium.[9]

Similarly, working at home is often disallowed because of the fear that if it is permitted, no one will ever be at the office. Yet for many people the very thought of such an arrangement is anathema. They enjoy the social aspects of work away from home, and many are concerned that they will be overlooked if they are not around. Further, not all homes are conducive to work. The distraction of very young children, for example, may preclude this possibility, and one woman who tried working at home had to give it up when she discovered that with the proximity of her refrigerator she had gained twenty pounds.

The fear that flexible arrangements will set a precedent with extensive and uncontrollable consequences is anchored in the presumed necessity for set procedures applied in uniform ways, whatever the personal circumstances might be. It denies the diversity of needs and desires that actually exists—the very diversity that the suggested flexibilities are meant to reflect.

To be sure, the definition of discrimination as disparate treatment reinforces tendencies toward strict uniformity. But as we have seen throughout this book—and as now included in the definition of discrimination—equal treatment may have disparate impact. Yet *the tendency to equate fairness with equality* is another source of resistance. Somehow it is not considered fair to have different arrangements for different people,[10] but people do have different personal circumstances and face different external constraints. We need to expand our views of what determines a legitimate personal concern beyond children and even beyond care in general, important as these are. Everyone has a private life, and everyone can benefit from flexibility based on individual circumstances.

Such an expanded view of fairness requires a shift in our thinking. Instead of conceiving of fairness in terms of equality, the thinking that underlies insurance would be more appropriate. We do not complain that we are not being treated fairly because we do not get sick and hence do not get the same benefits from our health insurance as our diseased colleagues. Why cannot working arrangements designed to suit individual circumstances be accepted in the same way?

For example, an American consulting company needed to send a team to do a job in London. One of the people it wanted to send had a small child. She was uniquely qualified for the job but found it difficult to consider leaving her child for the few months the engagement would take. The company arranged to have her fly back every weekend to be with her family; she accepted this arrangement and was at home while the rest of the team stayed in London and continued its work. Is this fair? Interestingly, the other women on the team had no complaints; they gladly put in the extra time because they could imagine a time when they would need such an arrangement and were happy to see their employer willing to accommodate employees in this way. In contrast, the men on the team were less sure that the arrangement was fair, seeing it instead as special treatment for women.

Such backlash[11] is perhaps an inevitable response to changing rules. It is certainly evident in the perceived loss of opportunity felt by white males in reaction to companies' affirmative action efforts. But in the improved world envisioned here, men would also benefit from company willingness to accommodate individual circumstances. Like the women above, they would view such an arrangement as an insurance available in their own future lives when the need or desire arose. And the company would gain by a reputation for caring about its workers that would establish it as an employer of choice for the most qualified and imaginative people starting a career.

Another example stems from a forward-looking computer company that provides part-time employees who work more than twenty hours per week with full benefits. Such an arrangement is very useful for people at certain periods in their lives, but when an employee shifts from a full-time to a part-time schedule, there may be work that is left undone. Despite the best intentions, this company has not considered other possible modifications that could deal with this difficulty, such as combining part-time employees into shared jobs or providing "floaters" (people or units trained to step in to fill the work of absent employees). Nor has it found a way to advance the careers of part-time employees, implicitly relegating them more or less permanently to a separate and secondary career track. Such modifications are not without cost, but the immediate costs of instituting such changes are considerably less than the long-run costs of *not* doing so. Moreover, such improved and more imaginative arrangements ought to be able to reflect the natural ebb and flow of work itself. Discontinuities exist in work flow as well as in people's lives, and it should be possible to accommodate both as long as the "chaos" of individualized and discontinuous arrangements is accepted as part of the necessary way of accomplishing organizational goals.

In organizations built on the acceptance of equal legitimacy of the needs of work and of workers' private lives, employees would take responsibility for high-quality and timely work. They would arrange individually or within teams for the appropriate allocation of assignments, time schedules, and location of work to guarantee this result. Companies in turn would "reengineer" the work process to ensure that demands on workers reflect only the basic requirements for reaching organizational goals.

Government support would also help. If employers were no longer responsible for all health costs, for example, they might be able to reconsider their policy of downsizing in order to cut costs. Over the last decade, American industry's response to competitive pressures by massive layoffs has led to a polarized world: a growing disparity between rich and poor, and an illogical division between those who are under- or unemployed and those who are working longer and longer hours.[12] Rather than companies downsizing and consequently expecting increased contributions from surviving staff, alternatives that share the work through reduced hours and compensation might be seen as mutually beneficial options. Such arrangements have been used in a number of European countries. Instead of responding to downturns by layoffs, only to have to rehire when demand again increases, companies in other countries are more likely to protect jobs and to ride out the fluctuations in other ways.[13]

There are also some movements in the United States toward this different organizational world. For example, when a strike at a parts factory hit the new GM Saturn plant in Tennessee, none of the workers (all of whom were on salary) were laid off, even though production was stopped within a few hours. The strike was settled soon thereafter, but one Saturn executive said that if it had been prolonged the company would have reduced everyone's pay—workers and managers alike— rather than lay people off, in order to keep intact its implicit agreement with the union for joint contribution to the success of the firm.

A different set of personal values is also at times in evidence. When Paul B. Kazarian was ousted despite success as the chairman of the Sunbeam-Oster Company, for example, there was speculation that his managers rebelled against his management style, including "his insistence that they carry beepers and work seven days a week."[14] Conversely, when the Los Angeles Department of Water and Power instituted a program for fathers (including support groups, workshops, and field trips) as part of its services to employees, its director of human resources reported turnover of 2 percent among participating employees, compared to 5 percent among nonparticipants.[15]

At Levi Strauss, the CEO was involved in a task force to implement the company's pledge in its mission statement for a "commitment to balanced personal and professional lives." As a result the company now provides long vacations, all Friday afternoons off, and a time-off-with-pay program that combines sick days with time off for other personal reasons. The firm's long-run goal is "to change ways of thinking so that work/family will be viewed not only as a program, but as the outgrowth of a philosophical perspective, a new way of doing business that ultimately contributes to the company's bottom line."[16]

Levi Strauss provides an array of alternative work schedules from job sharing to telecommuting, and they are aware of the career implications of using such alternatives. Their director of employment reports that

> There's nothing built into the system that says if you go onto an alternative work schedule, you're not a fast tracker. For example, Donna Goya, one of nine senior managers with the company, took a year off, worked part-time, did a job-share, and still earned a top management position. While I'm not aware of any men who have yet taken advantage of alternative work schedules, it's something that we're educating about and will come someday soon. These men are married to women who also have careers; the expectation today is that a child is raised by both parents, so we are now seeing men who are experiencing family demands at work.

The report also states that Goya (now Levi Strauss's full time director of personnel) used her two days off in the period of her three-day workweek as "a developmental tool for her subordinates. They took turns assuming her responsibilities."[17] The benefit of the arrangement therefore transcended her idiosyncratic, individual circumstance.

These examples go some way to meeting the needs of the future organizational world. They show that the integration of employees' private lives with the requirements of company work is possible. Whether equitable career outcomes will accompany such integration is still an open question, the answer to which will depend on the extent to which all employees—male and female, career ambitious and task oriented—feel free to take advantage of the policies provided.[18]

The ultimate goal is for companies to view these issues brought on by an increasingly diverse work force not as marginal problems, but as opportunities for productive change in the organization of work.[19] Companies need not embark on this path only for the common good; on the contrary, by being innovative in their response to employee needs, they necessarily have to rethink their accepted ways of doing work. Such an effort is likely to produce greater long-run productivity, as well as to enhance the overall commitment and responsibility of employees toward the organization's goals.

Allowing employees to withdraw some identification with paid work and to increase their involvement with community and family may also have less obvious positive consequences. In Chapter 3 I discussed the possibility of transferring the requirements of work to activities in the private sphere. But what about the other way around? Might there not be attributes acquired in personal life that could be usefully applied to the occupational world? Martha Chase, whose family story was portrayed in Interlude I, reported that "as an outgrowth of being a mother and having household responsibilities, I learned how to do things faster, [to] organize my time for things that have to be done, [and] to constantly reevaluate the priorities and plan ahead." These organizational skills, learned in her home, allowed her to be a valuable employee even though she put strict limits on her office presence.

Other skills could also transfer from private life to the accomplishment of organizational work. American companies, particularly as they move toward more empowered workers, are concerned about the lack of skills in the work force to ensure coordinated, team-oriented, interactive, and interdependent ways of working. But many of these same employees display these skills in their private lives. Perhaps if companies valued this other part of their employees' lives more fully, they would find such skills being applied also to occupational work.[20]

Finally, as I finish these pages, the United States has an administration in Washington more ready to assume some governmental responsibility for the basic social needs of the population. Such a national response, as noted earlier, might lift some of this burden from employers and make them freer to attend to the issues discussed in this book. The future welfare of the entire society may ultimately depend on their doing so.

NOTES

1. INTRODUCTION: THE WORLD WE LIVE IN

1. Joseph H. Boyett and Henry P. Conn, *Workplace 2000: The Revolution Reshaping American Business* (New York: Dutton, 1991), 40.

2. Ibid.

3. For a detailed discussion of the history of the relation of work and family, see Rosabeth Moss Kanter, *Work and Family in the United States* (New York: Russell Sage Foundation, 1977); and for a recent summary of research on the linkages between work and family, see Marianne A. Ferber and Brigid O'Farrell (with La Rue Allen), eds., *Work and Family: Policies for a Changing Work Force* (Washington: National Academy Press, 1991), chap. 3. For discussion by legal scholars of the relation between public and private life, see Nancy E. Dowd,

"Work and Family: The Gender Paradox and the Limitations of Discrimination Analysis in Restructuring the Workplace," *Harvard Civil Rights Civil Liberties Law Review* 24 (1989), 79–172; Frances E. Olsen, "The Family and the Market: A Study of Ideology and Legal Reform," *Harvard Law Review* 98 (1983), 1497–1578; and Joan C. Williams, "Deconstructing Gender," *Michigan Law Review* 87 (1989), 797–845. An early anthropological perspective is given in Michelle Z. Rosaldo and Louise Lamphere, eds., *Woman, Culture, and Society* (Stanford, CA: Stanford University Press, 1974), especially in Rosaldo, "Woman, Culture, and Society: A Theoretical Overview," 17–42.

4. The impact of these changes was captured initially in William B. Johnston and Arnold E. Packer, *Workforce 2000: Work and Workers for the Twenty-First Century* (Indianapolis: Hudson Institute, 1987). Because the summary to that study did not make clear that it dealt with *net* changes (entrants into the work force minus leavers) and because men are a much larger proportion of the leavers than of the entrants and the reverse is true for women, their projected "feminization" of the work force was dramatic. Though corrected in later analyses—for example, Howard N. Fullerton, Jr., "New Labor Force Projections, Spanning 1988 to 2000," *Monthly Labor Review* 112 (November 1989), 3–12; Lawrence Mishel and Ruy A. Teixeira, *The Myth of the Coming Labor Shortage: Jobs, Skills, and Incomes of America's Workforce 2000* (Washington, DC: Economic Policy Institute, 1991)—this projection entered the ongoing discourse and galvanized a number of leading companies into preparing for a very diversified work force. This response has certainly been helpful, but as will be seen, it also introduces unexpected difficulties.

5. Howard V. Hayghe, "Family Members in the Work Force," *Monthly Labor Review* 113 (March 1990), 14–19.

6. William J. Wiatrowski, "Family-Related Benefits in the Workplace," *Monthly Labor Review* 113 (March 1990), 28–33.

7. Sar A. Levitan and Elizabeth A. Conway, *Families in Flux: New Approaches to Meeting Workforce Challenges for Child, Elder, and Health Care in the 1990s* (Washington, DC: Bureau of National Affairs, 1990).

8. See Douglas W. Bray, Richard J. Campbell, and Donald L. Grant, *Formative Years in Business: A Long-Term AT & T Study of Managerial Lives* (New York: Wiley, 1974); and Ann Howard and Douglas W. Bray, *Managerial Lives in Transition: Advancing Age and Changing Times* (New York: Guilford, 1988).

9. Pauline Leinberger and Bruce Tucker, "The Sun Sets on the Silent Generation," *New York Times*, August 4, 1991, p. 11.

10. It should be pointed out that even though Taylor is the father of scientific management, he had some rather modern views. In his description of "systematizing the largest bicycle ball factory in this country," he reported on shortening the hours of the female workers and on the desirability of the state "when the girls have been properly selected and on the one hand such precautions have been taken as to guard against the possibility of overdriving them, while, on the other hand, the temptation to slight their work has been removed and the most favorable working conditions have been established." Frederick Winslow Taylor, *The Principles of Scientific Management* (New York: Harper, 1911), 93.

11. See also Jopseh F. Coates, Jennifer Jarratt, and John B. Mahaffie, *Future Work: Seven Critical Forces Reshaping Work and the Work Force in North America* (San Francisco: Jossey-Bass, 1990).

12. Leinberger and Tucker, "The Sun Sets on the Silent Generation."

13. Rosabeth Moss Kanter, *When Giants Learn to Dance: Mastering the Challenge of Strategy, Management, and Careers in the 1990s* (New York: Simon and Schuster, 1989).

14. Kanter, *When Giants Learn to Dance*; Boyett and Conn, *Workplace 2000*.

15. For a discussion of time, see Juliet B. Schor, "Americans Work Too Hard," *New York Times*, July 25, 1991, p. 21; and Kathleen Hirsch, "A New Vision of Corporate America," *Boston Globe Magazine*, April 21, 1991, pp. 16ff. The term *family workweek* comes from Levitan and Conway, *Families in Flux*.

16. Michael L. Dertouzos, Richard K. Lester, and Robert M. Solow, *Made in America: Regaining the Productive Edge* (Cambridge: MIT Press, 1989).

17. Ferber and O'Farrell, *Work and Family*.

2. ORGANIZATIONAL CONSTRAINTS

1. Rosabeth Moss Kanter, "Careers and the Wealth of Nations: A Macro-Perspective on the Structure and Implications of Career Forms," in *Handbook of Career Theory*, eds. Michael B. Arthur, Douglas T. Hall, and Barbara S. Lawrence (Cambridge, England: Cambridge University Press, 1989), 506–521.

Notes

2. Despite the fact that academic work has long shown this disjunction to exist—see, for example, Lotte Bailyn (with E. H. Schein), *Living with Technology: Issues at Mid-Career* (Cambridge: MIT Press, 1980); Edgar H. Schein, *Career Dynamics: Matching Individual and Organizational Needs* (Reading, MA: Addison-Wesley, 1978); Michael J. Driver, "Career Concepts: A New Approach to Career Research," in *Career Issues in Human Resource Management*, ed. Ralph Katz (Englewood Cliffs, NJ: Prentice-Hall, 1982), 23–32; C. Brooklyn Derr, *Managing the New Careerists* (San Francisco: Jossey-Bass, 1986); Gene W. Dalton and Paul H. Thompson, *Novations: Strategies for Career Management* (Glenview, IL: Scott, Foresman, 1986)—in many companies traditional, monolithic assumptions are still operative.

3. Rosabeth Moss Kanter, *Men and Women of the Corporation* (New York: Basic Books, 1977); see also Robert Jackall, *Moral Mazes: The World of Corporate Managers* (New York: Oxford University Press, 1988).

4. This example stems from Lotte Bailyn and John T. Lynch, "Engineering as a Life-Long Career: Its Meaning, Its Satisfactions, Its Difficulties," *Journal of Occupational Behaviour* 4 (1983), 263–283.

5. There were more women in the home-based group than in the office-based one. Nonetheless, statistical analysis showed that the locus of employment had a significant effect on these patterns of meaning even when gender was controlled. See Lotte Bailyn, "Toward the Perfect Workplace?" *Communications of the ACM* 32 (1989), 460–471.

6. This example stems from Lotte Bailyn, "Resolving Contradictions in Technical Careers," *Technology Review* (November/December 1982), 40–47. The often dysfunctional relationshp between design and manufacturing has recently been eloquently described in Robert J. Thomas, *What Machines Can't Do: Politics and Technology in the Industrial Enterprise* (Berkeley: University of California Press, in press).

7. W. Edwards Deming, *Out of the Crisis* (Cambridge: Center for Advanced Engineering Study, 1986), 24.

8. See Joseph A. Raelin, *The Clash of Cultures: Managers and Professionals* (Boston: Harvard Business School Press, 1986).

9. Kanter, in "Careers and the Wealth of Nations," defines this career as entrepreneurial, whereas Edgar H. Schein, in *Career Anchors: Discovering Your Real Values*, rev. ed. (San Diego: University Associates, 1990), presumes that people dedicated to sales have autonomy as a career anchor.

10. Lotte Bailyn, "Involvement and Accommodation in Technical Careers: An Inquiry into the Relation to Work at Mid-Career," in *Organizational Careers: Some New Perspectives*, ed. John Van Maanen (New York: Wiley International, 1977), 109–132.

11. See Schein, *Career Dynamics*. In later work, which included also data from women, there emerged a life-style anchor, where people's concerns and orientations could not be gauged if only orientations to occupational work were considered (see Robbe Burnstine, "Career Anchors of Management and Strategic Consultants," master's thesis, MIT, 1982). Though such orientations are more often found in women, they are by no means absent in men—and may increasingly exist for both women and men.

12. See Bailyn and Lynch, "Engineering as a Life-Long Career."

13. Paul Evans and Fernando Bartolome, *Must Success Cost So Much?* (London: Grant McIntyre, 1980).

14. Parts of this section are based on Lotte Bailyn, "The Hybrid Career: An Exploratory Study of Career Routes in R & D," *Journal of Engineering and Technology Management* 8 (1991), 1–14. Data and quotes stem from intensive semistructured interviews with fifteen to twenty people at all levels of the organization in each of five R & D labs (in the United States and the United Kingdom), all central facilities of large, successful corporations.

15. For a vivid description of what is involved in the move from independent contributor to manager see Linda A. Hill, *Becoming a Manager: Mastery of a New Identity* (Boston: Harvard Business School Press, 1992).

16. This example stems from Bailyn, "The Hybrid Career."

17. They are following what Kanter, in "Careers and the Wealth of Nations," calls a "professional" career.

18. The figures come from Karen A. Epstein, *Socialization Practices and Their Consequences: The Case of an Innovative Organization*, Sloan School of Management Working Paper 1502–83, MIT, 1983. For other analyses of the systematic difficulties with the dual ladder, see Hugh P. Gunz, "Dual Ladders in Research: A Paradoxical Organizational Fix," *R & D Management* 10 (1980), 113–118; Laurie M. Roth, *Critical Examination of the Dual Ladder Approach to Career Advancement* (New York: Center of Research in Career Development, Columbia University Graduate School of Business, 1982); Thomas J. Allen and Ralph Katz, "The Dual Ladder: Motivational Solution or Managerial Delusion? *R & D Management* 16 (1986), 185–197.

19. For example, Allen and his associates have shown that a relatively large group (between one-third and one-half of the R & D professionals they surveyed) say they are more interested in a series of challenging research projects than they are in promotion or advancement up either a managerial or technical ladder; Thomas J. Allen and Ralph Katz, "The Treble Ladder Revisited: Why Do Engineers Lose Interest in the Dual Ladder as They Grow Older? *International Journal of Vehicle Design* 12 (1991), 478–488; Karen A. Epstein, "The Dual Ladder: Realities of Technically-Based Careers," Ph.D. dissertation, MIT, 1986; Paul McKinnon, "Steady-State People: A Third Career Orientation," *Research Management* 30 (1987), 26–29.

20. This orientation is similar to what Schein, in *Career Anchors*, calls the career anchor of pure challenge, and what Derr refers to as the warrior; C. Brooklyn Derr, "More About Career Anchors," in *Work, Family, and the Career: New Frontiers in Theory and Research*, ed. C. Brooklyn Derr (New York: Praeger, 1980), 166–187. The difficulty of defining organizational procedures to fit this orientation is exemplified by the fact that it and the life-style anchor are the only ones for which Schein makes no organizational recommendations.

21. Kanter, "Careers and the Wealth of Nations."

22. For evidence of dissatisfaction, see R. Richard Ritti, *The Engineer in the Industrial Corporation* (New York: Columbia University Press, 1971); and Bailyn, *Living with Technology*. For evidence of decrement of performance, see Dalton and Thompson, *Novations*. Gary Jewkes, Paul Thompson, and Gene Dalton, "How to Stifle a Technical Organization in Ten Easy Steps," *Research Management* 22 (1979), 12–16 and Thomas J. Allen and Ralph Katz, "Managing Engineers and Scientists: Some New Perspectives," in *Human Resource Management in International Firms: Change, Globalization, Innovation*, eds. Paul Evans, Yves Doz, and Andre Laurent (London: Macmillan, 1989) discuss obsolescence, and stagnation is covered by Ralph Katz, "Managing Careers: The Influence of Job and Group Longevities," in *Career Issues in Human Resource Management*, ed. Ralph Katz (Englewood Cliffs, NJ: Prentice-Hall, 1982) and Bailyn, "Resolving Contradictions in Technical Careers."

23. See, for example, Luis R. Gomez-Mejia, David B. Balkin, and George T. Milkovich, "Rethinking Rewards for Technical Employees," *Organizational Dynamics* 18 (1990), 62–75.

24. Such movement could fit what Kanter, in "Careers and the Wealth of Nations," calls the entrepreneurial career and the people

whom Schein, in *Career Anchors,* identifies as having an entrepreneurial career anchor.

25. In the very different cultural context of Japanese companies, such movement is much more usual (see D. Eleanor Westney and Kiyonori Sakakibara, *Comparative Study of the Training, Careers, and Organization of Engineers in the Computer Industry in Japan and the United States,* MIT-Japan Science and Technology Program Working Paper 85-03, MIT, 1985). And according to one report, a number of Dutch companies try to stimulate it even though it is not part of official policy; E. J. Tuininga, "Social Management in Professional Organizations: Searching for New Impulses," *R & D Management* 20 (1990), 139–153.

3. INDIVIDUAL CONSTRAINTS

1. Rosabeth Moss Kanter, *Work and Family in the United States* (New York: Russell Sage Foundation, 1977).

2. On the whole one would expect an easier integration under conditions of overlap, but there may be exceptions. Perhaps the burnout associated with many in the helping professions—see Christina Maslach, *Burnout: The Cost of Caring* (Englewood Cliffs, NJ: Prentice-Hall, 1982)—is in part a result of too little difference between the demands of work and those of private life.

3. For descriptions of issues in the managerial career, see Hugh Gunz, *Careers and Corporate Cultures: Managerial Mobility in Large Corporations* (Oxford: Basil Blackwell, 1989); Linda A. Hill, *Becoming a Manager: Mastery of a New Identity* (Boston: Harvard Business School Press, 1992); Robert Jackall, *Moral Mazes: The World of Corporate Managers* (New York: Oxford University Press, 1988); and Rosabeth Moss Kanter, *Men and Women of the Corporation* (New York: Basic Books, 1977).

4. This definition of overload is based on Karl E. Weick, "The Twigging of Overload," in *People and Information,* ed. H. B. Pepinsky (New York: Pergamon, 1970), 67–129; and it is applied by him to managerial work in his review of Mintzberg; Karl E. Weick, "Review of *The Nature of Managerial Work* by Henry Mintzberg," *Administrative Science Quarterly* 19 (1974), 111–118.

5. For descriptions of managerial work, see John P. Kotter, *The General Managers* (New York: Free Press, 1982); Henry Mintzberg, *The Nature of Managerial Work* (New York: Harper and Row, 1973);

and Rosemary Stewart, *Choices for the Manager* (Englewood Cliffs, NJ: Prentice-Hall, 1982).

6. See James E. Rosenbaum, *Career Mobility in a Corporate Hierarchy* (Orlando, FL: Academic Press, 1984).

7. See, for example, Judy B. Rosener, "Ways Women Lead," *Harvard Business Review* (November-December 1990), 119–125; Marilyn Loden, *Feminine Leadership, or How to Succeed in Business Without Being One of the Boys* (New York: Times Books, 1985).

8. See Diana Werrell Tremblay, "An Exploratory Study of Dual-Career Couples in Corporate America," master's thesis, MIT, 1990.

9. Phyllis A. Wallace, *MBAs on the Fast Track: Career Mobility of Young Managers* (New York: Ballinger, 1989).

10. See also Amy Andrews and Lotte Bailyn, "Segmentation and Synergy: Two Models of Linking Work and Family," in *Men, Work and Family*, ed. Jane C. Hood (Newbury Park, CA: Sage, in press).

11. See Amy Andrews, *Flexible Working Schedules in High Commitment Organizations: A Challenge to the Emotional Norms?* Sloan School of Management Working Paper 3329-91-BPS, MIT, 1991; and Constance Perin, "The Moral Fabric of the Office: Panopticon Discourse and Schedule Flexibilities," in *Research in the Sociology of Organizations: Organizations and Professions*, eds. Pamela S. Tolbert and Stephen R. Barley (Greenwich, CT: JAI Press, 1991), 241–268.

12. Obvious exceptions are human resource specialists who deal with issues of individual or organizational development.

13. See Rosenbaum, *Career Mobility;* R. Richard Ritti, *The Engineer in the Industrial Corporation* (New York: Columbia University Press, 1971); and Lotte Bailyn (with E. H. Schein), *Living with Technology: Issues at Mid-Career* (Cambridge: MIT Press, 1980). More recent work, however, shows that besides this emphasis on "real" engineering, some engineers not only do but *like* to do more interpersonal, coordinating work; Leslie Perlow, "The Myth of 'Real Work': The Case of Engineering," Sloan School of Management, MIT, 1993. Such "invisible" work, though, is not easily absorbed into the typical engineering role.

14. These data stem from Lotte Bailyn, "Experiencing Technical Work: A Comparison of Male and Female Engineers," *Human Relations* 40 (1987), 299–312.

15. See Lawrence Schlesinger Kubie, "Some Unresolved Problems of the Scientific Career," *American Scientist* 41 (1953),

596–613; and idem, "Psychoneurotic Problems of the American Scientist," *Chicago Review* 8 (1954), 65–80.

16. Based on findings from the alumni study mentioned in Chapter 2.

17. Report of the Ad Hoc Committee on Family and Work, 1990.

18. For an interesting example, see Deborah M. Kolb, "Women's Work: Peacemaking in Organizations," in *Hidden Conflict in Organizations: Uncovering Behind-the-Scenes Disputes*, eds. Deborah M. Kolb and Jean M. Bartunek (Newbury Park, CA: Sage, 1992).

4. FAMILY AS AN EMERGING ISSUE FOR ORGANIZATIONS

1. Parts of this chapter are based on Lotte Bailyn, "Changing the Conditions of Work: Implications for Career Development," in *Career Development in the 1990s: Theory and Practice*, eds. David H. Montross and Christopher J. Shinkman (Springfield, IL: Charles C Thomas, 1992); and idem, "Changing the Conditions of Work: Responding to Increasing Work Force Diversity and New Family Patterns," in *Transforming Organizations*, eds. Thomas Kochan and Michael Useem (Oxford: Oxford University Press, 1992).

2. U.S. Department of Labor, *Child Care: A Workforce Issue*, Report of the Secretary's Task Force, Washington, DC, 1988.

3. Cheryl D. Hayes, John Palmer, and Martha Zaslow, eds., *Who Cares for America's Children: Child Care Policy for the 1990s*, Report of the Panel on Child Care Policy, Committee on Child Development Research and Public Policy. (Washington, DC: Commission on Behavioral and Social Sciences and Education, National Research Council, 1990).

4. William B. Johnston and Arnold E. Packer, *Workforce 2000: Work and Workers for the Twenty-First Century* (Indianapolis: Hudson Institute, 1987).

5. U.S. Department of Commerce, *Current Population Reports*, Special Studies Series, P-23, Number 159 (Washington, DC: Bureau of the Census, 1989).

6. U.S. Department of Labor, *Employment and Earnings* (Washington, DC: Bureau of Labor Statistics, 1988).

7. Ellen Galinsky, "The Implementation of Flexible Time and Leave Policies: Observations from European Employers," paper prepared for the Panel on Employer Policies and Working Families,

Committee on Women's Employment and Related Social Issues, Commission on Behavioral and Social Sciences and Education, National Research Council, Washington, DC, 1989.

8. Quoted in Cathy Trost, "Best Employers for Women and Parents," *Wall Street Journal,* November 30, 1987, p. 23.

9. For predictions under a number of different assumptions, see Howard N. Fullerton, Jr., "New Labor Force Projections, Spanning 1988 to 2000," *Monthly Labor Review* 112 (November 1989), 3–12.

10. See, for example, *Work and Family: A Changing Dynamic* (Washington, DC: Bureau of National Affairs, 1986); *Fundamentals of Employee Benefit Programs,* 3rd ed. (Washington, DC: Employee Benefit Research Institute, 1987); and Marianne A. Ferber and Brigid O'Farrell (with La Rue Allen), eds., *Work and Family: Policies for a Changing Work Force* (Washington, DC: National Academy Press, 1991).

11. That the perceived value of employees may itself be a function of an employee's gender and family position is analyzed in Joanne Martin, "Deconstructing Organizational Taboos: The Suppression of Gender Conflict in Organizations," *Organization Science* 1 (1990), 339–359.

12. See Juliet B. Schor, *The Overworked American: The Unexpected Decline of Leisure* (New York: Basic Books, 1991) for an extensive analysis of the changing hours of the U.S. work force.

13. Suzanne Gordon, "Men, Women and Work: Job Dissatisfaction Knows No Gender," *Boston Globe,* July 28, 1991, p. 68.

14. E. M. Fowler, "More Stress in the Workplace," *New York Times,* September 20, 1989, p. D22.

15. See, for example, Robert E. Weigand, "What's a Fair Day's Work?" *New York Times,* April 19, 1986, p. 27; and Dan Subotnik, "Productivity's Little Secret: Hard Work," *New York Times,* May 14, 1989, Business section, p. 2.

16. It is ironic that Japan is currently trying to induce its workers to take more vacation time and is putting in place a whole set of interrelated procedures in order to move to a five-day week ("Coming: The 5-Day Week for All," editorial, *Japan Times,* August 28, 1988, p. 18).

17. See, for example, Richard E. Walton, "From Control to Commitment: Transforming Work Force Management in the United States," in *The Uneasy Alliance: Managing the Productivity–Technology Dilemma,* eds. Kim B. Clark, Robert H. Hayes, and Christopher Lorenz (Boston: Harvard Business School Press, 1985), 237–265;

Edward E. Lawler III, *High-Involvement Management* (San Francisco: Jossey-Bass, 1990); Michael L. Dertouzos, Richard K. Lester, and Robert M. Solow, *Made in America: Regaining the Productive Edge* (Cambridge: MIT Press, 1989); and Rosabeth Moss Kanter, *When Giants Learn to Dance: Mastering the Challenge of Strategy, Management, and Careers in the 1990s* (New York: Simon and Schuster, 1989).

18. Ronald Dore, "Japan's Version of Managerial Capitalism," in *Transforming Organizations*, eds. Thomas A. Kochan and Michael Useem (New York: Oxford University Press, 1992), 17–26.

19. For men, in particular, the culturally valued commitment to work is already so strong that these new organizational demands will make it even more difficult for them to honor family commitments, the demand for which is also increasing; (see Stephen R. Marks, "Multiple Roles and Role Strain: Some Notes on Human Energy, Time and Commitment," *American Sociological Review* 42 (1977), 921–936. The dilemma that commitment creates is dealt with in chapter 6.

20. See, for example, *Work and Family: A Changing Dynamic*, and Fran Sussner Rodgers and Charles Rodgers, "Business and the Facts of Family Life," *Harvard Business Review* (November-December, 1989), 121–129.

21. Joan C. Williams, "Deconstructing Gender," *Michigan Law Review* 87 (1989), 797–845.

22. See Lenore J. Weitzman, *The Divorce Revolution: The Unexpected Social and Economic Consequences for Women and Children in America* (New York: Free Press, 1985); Terry J. Arendell, "Women and the Economics of Divorce in the Contemporary United States," *Signs* 13 (1987), 121–135.

23. See Rodgers and Rodgers, "Business and the Facts of Family Life."

24. See Edgar H. Schein, "How Can Organizations Learn Faster? The Challenge of Entering the Green Room," *Sloan Management Review* 34 (Winter 1993), 85–92; Gervase R. Bushe and A. B. (Rami) Shani, *Parallel Learning Structures: Increasing Innovation in Bureaucracies*, Addison-Wesley Series on Organization Development, eds. Edgar H. Schein and Richard Beckhard (Reading, MA: Addison-Wesley, 1991).

25. Lotte Bailyn, "Issues of Work and Family in Different National Contexts: How the United States, Britain, and Sweden Respond," *Human Resource Management* 31 (1992), 201–208.

Notes

26. See Judith D. Auerbach, *In the Business of Child Care: Employer Initiative and Working Women* (New York: Praeger, 1988).

27. Also affected is women's volunteer involvement in their communities at a time when, according to the Bush administration, "a thousand points of light" were to substitute for government involvement in such areas as education, health, and other community needs.

28. Lower-income women have long been in the work force, but it is less likely that their priorities have changed.

29. Ursula Huws, Werner B. Korte, and Simon Robinson, *Telework: Toward the Elusive Office* (Chichester, England: Wiley, 1990).

30. See Lotte Bailyn, "Toward the Perfect Workplace?" *Communications of the ACM* 32 (1989), 460–471.

31. Rhona Rapoport and Peter Moss, *Men and Women as Equals at Work: An Exploratory Study of Parental Leave in Sweden and Career Breaks in the U.K.,* Thomas Coram Research Unit Occasional Paper No. 11, University of London, 1990.

32. See Galinsky, "The Implementation of Flexible Time and Leave Policies."

33. Ariane Berthoin Antal and Dafna N. Izraeli, "Women in Management: An International Comparison," in *Women and Work*, vol. 4, ed. Ellen A. Fagenson (Beverly Hills, CA: Sage, 1993).

34. Rapoport and Moss, *Men and Women as Equals at Work.*

35. Nancy E. Dowd, "Envisioning Work and Family: A Critical Perspective on International Models," *Harvard Journal on Legislation* 26 (1989), 311–348.

36. See Janet Saltzman Chafetz, *Gender Equity: An Integrated Theory of Stability and Change* (Newbury Park, CA: Sage, 1990); Albert J. Mills and Stephen J. Murgatroyd, *Organizational Rules: A Framework for Understanding Organizational Action* (Milton Keynes, England: Oxford University Press, 1991).

37. Virginia E. Schein, "The Work–Family Interface: Challenging Corporate Convenient," paper presented at the annual convention of the American Psychological Association, Boston, August 1990.

38. See, for example, Kathleen Hirsch, "A new vision of corporate America," *Boston Globe Magazine,* April 21, 1991, pp. 16ff.

39. See Constance Perin, "The Moral Fabric of the Office: Panopticon Discourse and Schedule Flexibilities," in *Research in the Sociology of Organizations: Organizations and Professions,* eds. Pamela S. Tolbert and Stephen R. Barley (Greenwich, CT: JAI Press, 1991), 241–268.

40. See Bailyn, "Changing the Conditions of Work: Implications for Career Development."

41. See Phyllis A. Wallace, ed., *Equal Employment Opportunity and the AT & T Case* (Cambridge: MIT Press, 1976).

5. RETHINKING TIME AND AUTONOMY

1. Time has long been a subject of study, and the buying and selling of time (its "commodification") has been seen as a distinctive characteristic of industrial capitalism; Anthony Giddens, *The Constitution of Society: Outline of the Theory of Structuration* (Cambridge, England: Polity Press, 1984). Recently there have also appeared a number of books analyzing time from the point of view of different social science disciplines, for example, Elliott Jaques, *The Form of Time* (New York: Craw, Russak, 1982); Frank A. Dubinskas, ed., *Making Time: Ethnographies of High-Technology Organizations* (Philadelphia: Temple University Press, 1988); Joseph E. McGrath, ed., *The Social Psychology of Time: New Perspectives* (Newbury Park, CA: Sage, 1988); Michael Young, *The Metronomic Society: Natural Rhythms and Human Timetables* (London: Thames and Hudson, 1988); Michael Young and Tom Schuller, eds., *The Rhythms of Society* (London: Routledge, 1988); and Eviatar Zerubavel, *Hidden Rhythms: Schedules and Calendars in Social Life* (Chicago: University of Chicago Press, 1981).

2. Parts of this chapter are based on Lotte Bailyn, "Freeing Work from the Constraints of Location and Time," *New Technology, Work and Employment* 3 (1988), 143–152; idem, "Toward the Perfect Workplace?" *Communications of the ACM* 32 (1989), 460–471; and idem, "Changing the Conditions of Work: Responding to Increasing Work Force Diversity and New Family Patterns," in *Transforming Organizations,* eds. Thomas Kochan and Michael Useem (Oxford: Oxford University Press, 1992).

3. See Bailyn, "Toward the Perfect Workplace?"

4. Penny Miles, "Hi-Tech Key to a Work Revolution," *Cambridge* [England] *Evening News,* August 21, 1987, p. 25.

5. Further corroboration of the difficulty of thinking about time in these less conventional ways came from the reaction of a group of managers who heard this story. The suggestion that the employee ought to be able to watch the game was greeted with incredulous laughter.

6. These quotes, and those to follow, are taken from intensive in-

terviews with managers and engineers in the engineering division of a high-tech manufacturing company, as part of an ongoing study on the relation of work process to employees' family needs. This study is supported by the Ford Foundation, Grant 910-1036.

7. In a classic article, Marks demonstrates that the experience of time is a cultural construction and that the experience of its scarcity is embedded in the separation of spheres, the activities of which are differentially valued; Stephen R. Marks, "Multiple Roles and Role Strain: Some Notes on Human Energy, Time and Commitment," *American Sociological Review* 42 (1977), 921–936.

8. The quote is from Marie Jahoda, *Employment and Unemployment: A Social-Psychological Analysis* (Cambridge, England: Cambridge University Press, 1982). See also David Fryer and Philip Ullah, eds., *Unemployed People: Social and Psychological Perspectives* (Milton Keynes, England: Open University Press, 1987); and Dubinskas, *Making Time.*

9. Janice R. Kelly and Joseph E. McGrath, "Effects of Time Limits and Task Types on Task Performance and Interaction of Four-Person Groups," *Journal of Personality and Social Psychology* 49 (1980), 395–407.

10. For a summary of these experiments, see Allen C. Bluedorn and Robert B. Dernhardt, "Time and Organizations," *Journal of Management* 14 (1988), 299–320.

11. Personal communication.

12. Visibility is another proxy signal used by organizations that may be outdated, for it is not clear that continuous presence really is required in an age of knowledge-intensive work and the availability of technology for information and communication. Insistence on visibility, like time, is a way to control employees' careers, and such control may be anchored in outdated ways of managing; see Peter F. Drucker, "The Futures That Have Already Happened," *Economist,* October 21, 1989, pp. 19ff.; Brian Dumaine, "What the Leaders of Tomorrow See," *Fortune,* July 3, 1989, pp. 48ff.; James R. Houghton, "The Age of the Hierarchy Is Over," *New York Times,* September 24, 1989, p. 3.

13. See Ronald Edsforth, "Germans Shorten Workweek for Success," *New York Times,* June 22, 1992, p. A16.

14. See, for example, Allan R. Cohen and Herman Gadon, *Alternative Work Schedules: Integrating Individual and Organizational Needs* (Reading, MA: Addison-Wesley, 1978); Simcha Ronen,

Alternative Work Schedules: Selecting, Implementing, and Evaluating (Homewood, IL: Dow Jones-Irwin, 1984).

15. Juliet B. Schor, *The Overworked American: The Unexpected Decline of Leisure* (New York: Basic Books, 1991).

16. Barbara Presley Noble, "Benefits? For Part-Timers?" *New York Times,* August 16, 1992, Business section, p. 23.

17. Quoted in Barbara Schwarz Vanderkolk and Arid Armstrong Young, *The Work and Family Revolution: How Companies Can Keep Employees Happy and Business Profitable* (New York: Facts on File, 1991), 87.

18. Quoted in Felice N. Schwartz (with Jean Zimmerman), *Breaking with Tradition: Women and Work, the New Facts of Life* (New York: Time Warner, 1992), 184.

19. Jolie Solomon and John W. Mashek, "Billionaire with Itch for Big Game," *Boston Sunday Globe,* April 12, 1992, pp. 1, 14.

20. Constance Perin, "The Moral Fabric of the Office: Panopticon Discourse and Schedule Flexibilities," in *Research in the Sociology of Organizations: Organizations and Professions,* eds. Pamela S. Tolbert and Stephen R. Barley (Greenwich, CT: JAI Press, 1991), 241–268.

21. Paul Blyton, John Hassard, Stephen Hill, and Ken Starkey, *Time, Work and Organization* (London: Routledge, 1989); Ken Starkey, "Time and Professionalism: Disputes Concerning the Nature of Contract," *British Journal of Industrial Relations* 27 (1989), 375–395.

22. Starkey, "Time and Professionalism."

23. The AdeltaT technique is designed expressly for this purpose.

24. Murray Melbin, "The Colonization of Time," in *Human Activity and Time Geography,* eds. Tommy Carlstein, Don Parkes, and Nigel Thrift (New York: Wiley, 1978), 100.

25. George Stalk, Jr., "Time—the Next Source of Competitive Advantage," *Harvard Business Review* (July-August 1988), 41–51.

26. See J. Richard Hackman and Greg R. Oldham, *Work Redesign* (Reading, MA: Addison-Wesley, 1980).

27. See Lotte Bailyn, "Autonomy in the Industrial R & D Lab," *Human Resource Management* 24 (1985), 129–146.

28. Pelz and Andrews, for example, also found that scientists prefer freedom and control regarding the conditions of their work over autonomy to define their own research agenda; Donald C. Pelz and Frank M. Andrews, *Scientists in Organizations: Productive Climates for*

Research and Development, rev. ed. (Ann Arbor: Institute for Social Research, University of Michigan, 1976).

29. See Nina Toren, "Scientific Autonomy East and West: A Comparison of the Perceptions of Soviet and United States Scientists," *Human Relations* 32 (1979), 643–657; Anna-Maria Garden, GDS Consultants, London, personal communication.

30. See Ellen J. Langer, *The Psychology of Control* (Beverly Hills, CA: Sage, 1983); Edgar H. Schein, *Organizational Psychology,* 3rd ed. (Englewood Cliffs, NJ: Prentice-Hall, 1980).

31. The information for this example stems from Phillip Judkins, David West, and John Drew, *Networking in Organisations: The Rank Xerox Experiment* (Aldershot, England: Gower, 1985); Phillip Judkins, "Towards New Patterns of Work—the Rank Xerox Networking Experiment," *European Management Journal* 4 (1986), 192–196; Derek Homby, "Can We Teach Ourselves to Change?" *Royal Bank of Scotland Review* (September 1986), 14–21; and some informal discussions with the people involved. Rank Xerox is also described in Francis Kinsman, *The Telecommuters* (Chichester, England: Wiley, 1987).

32. Michael Dixon, "Jobs: How to Get the Best from Skilled Professionals," *Financial Times,* April 10, 1991, p. 15.

33. Sweden in general has a very high absentee rate, something on the order of 25 percent. One company, however, found that by increasing the control of its employees over the conditions of work it reduced its absentee rate from 30 percent to 5 percent (personal communication).

34. Perin, "The Moral Fabric of the Office."

35. Just recently the Communitarian Network, founded by the sociologist Amitai Etzioni, urged Americans to spend less time on their jobs and more with their families, particularly their children ("Americans Urged to Increase Time with Family, Work Less," *Boston Globe,* November 18, 1992, p. 17).

6. RETHINKING COMMITMENT AND EQUITY

1. This section was written with the assistance of Amy Andrews, whose working paper *Flexible Working Schedules in High Commitment Organizations: A Challenge to the Emotional Norms?* (Sloan School of Management Working Paper 3329-91-BPS, MIT, 1991) was prepared for this project. Her data and analysis are quoted in relevant parts

throughout this section. Her authorship is identified at the relevant points.

2. Ibid., 29.

3. See John Van Maanen and Gideon Kunda, " 'Real Feelings': Emotional Expression and Organizational Culture," in *Research in Organizational Behavior,* Vol. 11, eds. Barry M. Staw and Larry L. Cummings (Greenwich, CT: JAI Press, 1989), 43–103 for other examples of companies co-opting the full emotional involvement of their employees.

4. This example stems from Andrews, *Flexible Working Schedules,* 36–37.

5. NCJW Center for the Child Reports, "Accommodating Pregnancy in the Workplace" (November 1987) and "Employer Supports for Child Care" (August 1988), National Council of Jewish Women, New York.

6. This way of looking at commitment is more fully explicated in the next chapter.

7. Dennis C. Kinlaw, *Coaching for Commitment: Managerial Strategies for Obtaining Superior Performance* (San Diego: University Associates, 1989), 5, italics added.

8. See Robert Jackall, *Moral Mazes: The World of Corporate Managers* (New York: Oxford University Press, 1988).

9. Andrews, *Flexible Working Schedules,* 22.

10. See, for example, Ray Stata, "Organizational Learning: The Key to Management Innovation," *Sloan Management Review* 30 (Spring 1989), 63–74; Peter M. Senge, *The Fifth Discipline: The Art and Practice of the Learning Organization* (New York: Doubleday/ Currency, 1990); Edgar H. Schein, "How Can Organizations Learn Faster? The Challenge of Entering the Green Room," *Sloan Management Review* 34 (Winter 1993), 85–92.

11. According to Richard E. Walton, "From Control to Commitment: Transforming Work Force Management in the United States," in *The Uneasy Alliance: Managing the Productivity–Technology Dilemma,* eds. Kim B. Clark, Robert H. Hayes, and Christopher Lorenz (Boston: Harvard Business School Press, 1985), 237–265, the theme of the control model of management—the traditional type of organizational structure—is "to establish order, exercise control, and achieve efficiency in the application of the work force" (p. 243). The theme of the commitment model, in contrast, is "to first elicit employee commitment and then to expect effective-

ness and efficiency to follow as second-order consequences" (p. 245). Key aspects of systems designed around commitment are participation, open communication, and mutual trust. They require a flat structure with enriched jobs and an egalitarian environment; Edward E. Lawler III, *High-Involvement Management* (San Francisco: Jossey-Bass, 1990). Procedures that support such a system are skills-based pay, gain and profit sharing, and group self-management and accountability; Walton, "From Control to Commitment," Richard E. Walton and J. Richard Hackman, "Groups under Contrasting Management Strategies," in *Designing Effective Work Groups,* ed. Paul S. Goodman and Associates (San Francisco: Jossey-Bass, 1986), 186–201.

12. See Lotte Bailyn, "Involvement and Accommodation in Technical Careers: An Inquiry into the Relation to Work at Mid-Career," in *Organizational Careers: Some New Perspectives,* ed. John Van Maanen (New York: Wiley International, 1977).

13. This distinction has been the source of much legal confusion, as the treatises on the difference between differential treatment and differential impact in applying equal opportunity legislation make clear; for example, Joan C. Williams, "Deconstructing Gender," *Michigan Law Review* 87 (1989), 797–845; Wendy W. Williams, "Equality's Riddle: Pregnancy and the Equal Treatment/Special Treatment Debate," *New York University Review of Law & Social Change* 13 (1984–85), 325–380; Nancy E. Dowd, "Work and Family: The Gender Paradox and the Limitations of Discrimination Analysis in Restructuring the Workplace," *Harvard Civil Rights Civil Liberties Law Review* 24 (1989), 79–172.

14. The just distribution of rewards has received eloquent attention from philosophers through the ages. It also depends on context. In the United States, for example, rewards in the workplace are said to be distributed according to performance or merit. In contrast, such a distributive principle is specifically rejected in the decisions on organ transplants. Scully, however, questions whether these domains are really so different, or whether the objections to merit in the transplant case might not also apply to the work situation; Maureen Scully, "Organs and Organizations: Can Objections to Merit-Based Distribution of Organs Be Used to Inform Objections to Merit-Based Distribution of Jobs and Incomes?" Sloan School of Management, MIT, July 1992.

15. A recent analysis of inequality in work organizations con-

cludes that an equitable distribution of rewards according to work achievement is systematically *not* possible under current conditions of employment; Claus Offe, *Industry and Inequality: The Achievement Principle in Work and Social Status* (London: Edward Arnold, 1976). This analysis claims that personnel practices—recruitment, promotion, permission for flexiblility, and so forth—are necessarily based on symbolic substitutes for performance (see also Van Maanen and Kunda, " 'Real Feelings' ").

16. I am grateful to Nancy Katz for telling me about this effort. See Peter Gumpert, Frederick M. Gordon, Kathryn R. Welch, Gregory Offringa, and Nancy Katz, "Toward a Rawlsean System of Distributive Justice: Effects of Reward Distribution Systems on Performance, Behavior and Psychological Orientation," Institute for Work Democracy, Boston.

17. John Rawls, *A Theory of Justice* (Cambridge: Harvard University Press, 1971), as summarized in Amartya Sen, *Inequality Reexamined* (Cambridge: Harvard University Press, 1992).

18. Paul Atkinson and Sara Delamont, "Professions and Powerlessness: Female Marginality in the Learned Occupations," *Sociological Review* 38 (1990), 90–110. In their analysis of the marginality of women in the professions, Atkinson and Delamont use a similar distinction (based on Janous and Peloille) between two dimensions of professional roles: their indeterminacy—"the 'hidden curriculum' of job performance: all the tacit, implicit, unexamined" issues—and their technicity—"the explicit, rule-governed, codified part of a job" (p. 95). Like Offe, they comment on the increasing emphasis on "indeterminacy" brought about by changes in technological and social conditions, and on the inequities such an emphasis introduces in the distribution of professional rewards.

19. This is what Kanter calls "homosocial reproduction"; Rosabeth Moss Kanter, *Men and Women of the Corporation* (New York: Basic Books, 1977).

20. I am grateful to Rhona Rapoport for helpful and enlightening discussions on this topic. I am aware that I am dealing with this topic as isolated from such other differences as race and ethnicity. For a more inclusive framework, see, for example, Ella Louise Bell and Stella M. Nkomo, *Women in Management Research: Toward a New Framework*, Sloan School of Management Working Paper 3464-92, MIT, August 1992.

21. See, for example, Heidi I. Hartmann, ed., *Comparable Worth:*

New Directions for Research (Washington, DC: National Academy Press, 1985); *A Report on the Glass Ceiling Initiative* (Washington, DC: U.S. Department of Labor, 1991).

22. Andrews, *Flexible Working Schedules,* 16.

23. Anne S. Miner, "Structural Evolution Through Idiosyncratic Jobs: The Potential for Unplanned Learning." *Organization Science* 1 (1990), 195–210.

24. See Phyllis A. Wallace, *MBAs on the Fast Track: Career Mobility of Young Managers* (New York: Ballinger, 1989); Mary S. Couming, "Exploring the 'Glass Ceiling': A Comparison of Career Enablers and Barriers for Female and Male Middle Managers," master's thesis, MIT, 1988.

25. Fishkin has shown how "background inequalities"—inequalities stemming from differences in developmental opportunities—systematically undermine the principles underlying equal opportunity in the competition for occupational positions. But this logical analysis does not preclude, according to Fishkin, many changes that could be instituted to equalize the life chances of the country's populace; James S. Fishkin, *Justice, Equal Opportunity, and the Family* (New Haven: Yale University Press, 1983). In the same way, though the goals of productivity, gender equity, and family care may not form a logically feasible set, given present circumstances there is much that can be done to equalize the constraints between the sexes.

26. For example, Arlie Hochschild (with Anne Machung), *The Second Shift: Working Parents and the Revolution at Home* (New York: Viking, 1989); Rhona Rapoport and Peter Moss, *Men and Women as Equals at Work: An Exploratory Study of Parental Leave in Sweden and Career Breaks in the U.K.*, Thomas Coram Research Unit Occasional Paper No. 11, University of London, 1990.

27. Andrews, *Flexible Working Schedules,* 38.

7. PATHWAYS TO CHANGE

1. See, for example, Thomas A. Kochan and Michael Useem, eds., *Transforming Organizations* (New York: Oxford University Press, 1992).

2. Clearly, trust is critical. See Diego Gambetta, "Can We Trust Trust?" in *Trust: Making and Breaking Cooperative Relations,* ed. Diego Gambetta (New York: Basil Blackwell, 1988), 213–237; Constance Perin, "The Moral Fabric of the Office: Panopticon

Discourse and Schedule Flexibilities," in *Research in the Sociology of Organizations: Organizations and Professions,* eds. Pamela S. Tolbert and Stephen R. Barley (Greenwich, CT: JAI Press, 1991), 241–268.

3. Parts of this chapter are based on Lotte Bailyn, "Changing the Conditions of Work: Implications for Career Development," in *Career Development in the 1990s: Theory and Practice,* eds. David H. Montross and Christopher J. Shinkman (Springfield, IL: Charles C Thomas, 1992).

4. James E. Rosenbaum, *Career Mobility in a Corporate Hierarchy* (Orlando, FL: Academic Press, 1984).

5. See Lotte Bailyn, "The 'Slow Burn' Way to the Top: Some Thoughts on the Early Years in Organizational Careers," in *Work, Family, and the Career: New Frontiers in Theory and Research,* ed. C. Brooklyn Derr (New York: Praeger, 1980); Hugh Gunz, *Careers and Corporate Cultures: Managerial Mobility in Large Corporations* (Oxford: Basil Blackwell, 1989).

6. Lotte Bailyn, "Freeing Work from the Constraints of Location and Time," *New Technology, Work and Employment* 3 (1988), 143–152.

7. See John Van Maanen and Edgar H. Schein, "Toward a Theory of Organizational Socialization," in *Research in Organizational Behavior,* vol. 1, ed. Barry M. Staw (Greenwich, CT: JAI Press, 1979), 209–269.

8. See Karl E. Weick, "Organization Design: Organizations as Self-Designing Systems," *Organizational Dynamics* (Autumn 1977), 31–46; Karl E. Weick and Lisa R. Berlinger, "Career Improvisation in Self-Designing Organizations," in *Handbook of Career Theory,* eds. Michael B. Arthur, Douglas T. Hall, and Barbara S. Lawrence (Cambridge, England: Cambridge University Press, 1989).

9. See, for example, R. Roosevelt Thomas, "From Affirmative Action to Affirming Diversity," *Harvard Business Review* (March-April, 1990), 107–117.

10. *Binder Kadeer: Consultation in the Company,* Program on Negotiation Clearinghouse, Harvard Law School, Cambridge.

11. *Black Caucus Groups at Xerox Corporation* (A and B), Harvard Business School Cases 9-491-047 and 9-491-048.

12. There is an interesting parallel here to the Japanese principle of *kaizen,* where continuous improvement is achieved by seeing problems and disruptions not as difficulties to be avoided but as opportunities for learning; John Paul MacDuffie, "Beyond Mass Production?

171

Flexible Production Systems and Manufacturing Performance in the World Auto Industry," Ph.D. dissertation, MIT, 1991.

13. See, for example, Richard E. Walton, "From Control to Commitment: Transforming Work Force Management in the United States," in *The Uneasy Alliance: Managing the Productivity–Technology Dilemma,* eds. Kim B. Clark, Robert H. Hayes, and Christopher Lorenz (Boston: Harvard Business School Press, 1985), 237–265.

14. See, for example, Paula I. Robbins, *Successful Midlife Career Change: Self-Understanding and Strategies for Action* (New York: AMACOM, 1978).

15. C. Brooklyn Derr, "Career Switching and Career Strategies among U.S. Naval Officers," Technical Report, Naval Postgraduate School, Monterey, CA, 1979.

16. Seymour B. Sarason, *Work, Aging, and Social Change: Professionals and the One Life–One Career Imperative* (New York: Free Press, 1977).

17. Lotte Bailyn (with E. H. Schein), *Living with Technology: Issues at Mid-Career* (Cambridge: MIT Press, 1980).

18. Bill Friedman, quoted in Kathleen Hirsch, "A New Vision of Corporate America," *Boston Globe Magazine,* April 21, 1991, p. 50.

19. See Rosenbaum, *Career Mobility.*

20. Parts of this section are based on Lotte Bailyn, "Issues of work and family in organizations: Responding to social diversity," in *Working with Careers,* eds. Michael B. Arthur, Lotte Bailyn, Daniel J. Levinson, and Herbert A. Shepard (New York: Center for Research in Career Development, Columbia University, 1984); and idem, "Changing the Conditions of Work: Implications for Career Development."

21. See, for example, Hugh P. Gunz, "Dual Ladders in Research: A Paradoxical Organizational Fix," *R & D Management* 10 (1980), 113–118; Laurie M. Roth, *Critical Examination of the Dual Ladder Approach to Career Advancement,* (New York: Center of Research in Career Development, Columbia University Graduate School of Business, 1982); Karen A. Epstein, "The Dual Ladder: Realities of Technically-Based Careers," Ph.D. dissertation, MIT, 1986; Thomas J. Allen and Ralph Katz, "The Dual Ladder: Motivational Solution or Managerial Delusion?" *R & D Management* 16 (1986), 185–197; Ralph Katz, Michael L. Tushman, and Thomas J. Allen, "Exploring the Dynamics of Dual Ladders," in *Advances in the Management of Technology,* vol. 1, eds. Luis Gomez-Mejia and Michael W. Lawless (Greenwich, CT: JAI Press, 1992).

22. It is of interest to note that in flexible production systems, based on the Japanese model, both compensation and seniority are decoupled from task; MacDuffie, "Beyond Mass Production?"

23. See Chapter 5.

24. With the emphasis by total quality management (TQM) on meeting customer requirements as a first priority, I have an image of *cascading inefficiencies* throughout the economy. Each supplier meets the demands of its customers with no thought as to whether they are legitimate, instead of demanding that requirements be pared down to their most basic and efficient necessity.

8. ENVISIONING THE FUTURE

1. See Lotte Bailyn, "Patterened Chaos in Human Resource Management," *Sloan Management Review* 34 (Winter 1993), 77–83.

2. See Peter M. Senge, *The Fifth Discipline: The Art and Practice of the Learning Organization* (New York: Doubleday/Currency, 1990); Edgar H. Schein, "How Can Organizations Learn Faster? The Challenge of Entering the Green Room," *Sloan Management Review* 34 (Winter 1993), 85–92.

3. A description given by the physicist Joseph Ford of the Georgia Institute of Technology—an early proponent and contributor to chaos theory—as quoted in James Gleick, *Chaos: Making a New Science* (New York: Viking, 1987), 306.

4. I am indebted to Joyce Fletcher for this reformulation.

5. "Managing Maternity Leaves Can Be Easy," *USA Today,* February 26, 1992, p. 11A.

6. Jeffrey L. Bradach, "The Organization and Management of Chains: Owning, Franchising, and the Plural Form," Doctoral dissertation, Harvard Business School, 1992.

7. Douglas Murray McGregor, *The Human Side of Enterprise* (New York: McGraw-Hill, 1960), 33–34.

8. Robert W. White, "Motivation Reconsidered: The Concept of Competence," *Psychological Review* 66 (1959), 297–333; Edward L. Deci, *Intrinsic Motivation* (New York: Plenum, 1975); Mihaly Csikszentmihalyi, *Beyond Boredom and Anxiety* (San Francisco: Josssey-Bass, 1975). See also Robert E. Lane, *The Market Experience* (Cambridge, England: Cambridge University Press, 1991).

9. "Domestic Partner Coverage," Massachusetts Association of HMOs, June 1992.

10. In fact, there have long been "inequalities" in relations with employees. For example, health benefits favor married people with children; in most plans, a couple without children pays the same amount as a couple with four (or more) children.

11. Susan Faludi, *Backlash: The Undeclared War Against American Women* (New York: Crown, 1991).

12. See Bennet Harrison and Barry Bluestone, *The Great U-Turn: Corporate Restructuring and the Polarizing of America* (New York: Basic Books, 1988); Juliet B. Schor, *The Overworked American: The Unexpected Decline of Leisure* (New York: Basic Books, 1991).

13. According to research at the National Bureau of Economic Research on the world's leading industrialized nations, the United States stands out as the country most likely to translate fluctuations in demand into worker layoffs; Frank R. Lichtenberg, "In a Downturn, Cut Profits Before Jobs," *New York Times,* February 16, 1992, Business Section, p. 13.

14. Adam Bryant, "Ouster at Sunbeam Sets Wall Street Abuzz," *New York Times,* January 12, 1993, p. D1.

15. Quoted and reported in Charlene Marmer Solomon, "Work/Family Ideas That Break Boundaries," *Personnel Journal* (October 1992), 112–117.

16. Quoted and reported in Christine Vogel, "Levi Strauss and Co.—A work/family program in action," *Family Resource Coalition Report* 11, no. 2 (1992), 4–5.

17. Quoted and reported in Barbara Schwarz Vanderkolk and Arid Armstrong Young, *The Work and Family Revolution: How Companies Can Keep Employees Happy and Business Profitable* (New York: Facts on File, 1991).

18. Such freedom will only come if there is also equity within the family, a topic eloquently discussed in Susan Moller Okin, *Justice, Gender, and the Family* (New York: Basic Books, 1989).

19. Certain divisions of the Xerox Corporation are trying this approach, and it will be instructive to see the results of those experiments.

20. Joyce Fletcher introduced this theme into our ongoing project. See Joyce Fletcher, "Feminist Standpoint Research and Management Science: Castrating the Female Advantage," Department of Cooperative Education, Northeastern University, Boston; Leslie Perlow, "The Myth of 'Real Work': The Case of Engineering," Sloan School of Management, MIT, January 1993.

BIBLIOGRAPHY

Andrews, Amy, and Lotte Bailyn. Segmentation and synergy: Two models of linking work and family. In *Men, Work and Family*, ed. Jane C. Hood. Newbury Park, CA: Sage, in press.

Arthur, Michael B., Lotte Bailyn, Daniel J. Levinson, and Herbert A. Shepard. 1984. *Working with careers*. New York: Center for Research in Career Development, Columbia University.

Arthur, Michael B., Douglas T. Hall, and Barbara S. Lawrence. 1989. *Handbook of career theory*. Cambridge, England: Cambridge University Press.

Atkinson, Paul, and Sara Delamont. 1990. Professions and powerlessness: Female marginality in the learned occupations. *Sociological Review* 38: 90–110.

Bibliography

Auerbach, Judith D. 1988. *In the business of child care: Employer initiative and working women.* New York: Praeger.

Bailyn, Lotte. 1977. Involvement and accommodation in technical careers: An inquiry into the relation to work at mid-career. In *Organizational careers: Some new perspectives,* ed. John Van Maanen. New York: Wiley International.

Bailyn, Lotte (with E. H. Schein). 1980. *Living with technology: Issues at mid-career.* Cambridge: MIT Press.

Bailyn, Lotte. 1980. The "slow burn" way to the top: Some thoughts on the early years in organizational careers. In *Work, family, and the career: New frontiers in theory and research,* ed. C. Brooklyn Derr. New York: Praeger.

Bailyn, Lotte. 1985. Autonomy in the industrial R & D lab. *Human Resource Management* 24: 129–146.

Bailyn, Lotte. 1987. Experiencing technical work: A comparison of male and female engineers. *Human Relations* 40: 299–312.

Bailyn, Lotte. 1989. Toward the perfect workplace? *Communications of the ACM* 32: 460–471.

Bailyn, Lotte, and John T. Lynch. 1983. Engineering as a life-long career: Its meaning, its satisfactions, its difficulties. *Journal of Occupational Behaviour* 4: 263–283.

Bluedorn, Allen C., and Robert B. Denhardt. 1988. Time and organizations. *Journal of Management* 14: 299–320.

Blyton, Paul, John Hassard, Stephen Hill, and Ken Starkey. 1989. *Time, work and organization.* London: Routledge.

Dowd, Nancy E. 1989. Work and family: The gender paradox and the limitations of discrimination analysis in restructuring the workplace. *Harvard Civil Rights Civil Liberties Law Review* 24: 79–172.

Dubinskas, Frank A. 1988. *Making time: Ethnographies of high-technology organizations.* Philadelphia: Temple University Press.

Evans, Paul, and Fernando Bartolome. 1980. *Must success cost so much?* London: Grant McIntyre.

Bibliography

Ferber, Marianne A., and Brigid O'Farrell (with La Rue Allen). 1991. *Work and family: Policies for a changing work force.* Washington, DC: National Academy Press.

Fishkin, James S. 1983. *Justice, equal opportunity, and the family.* New Haven: Yale University Press.

Googins, Bradley K. 1991. *Work/family conflicts: Private lives—public responses.* New York: Auburn House.

Gunz, Hugh. 1989. *Careers and corporate cultures: Managerial mobility in large corporations.* Oxford: Basil Blackwell.

Handy, Charles. 1985. *The future of work: A guide to a changing society.* Oxford: Basil Blackwell.

Hill, Linda A. 1992. *Becoming a manager: Mastery of a new identity.* Boston: Harvard Business School Press.

Hochschild, Arlie (with Anne Machung). 1989. *The second shift: Working parents and the revolution at home.* New York: Viking.

Jackall, Robert. 1988. *Moral mazes: The world of corporate managers.* New York: Oxford University Press.

Johnston, William B., and Arnold E. Packer. 1987. *Workforce 2000: Work and workers for the twenty-first century.* Indianapolis: Hudson Institute.

Kanter, Rosabeth Moss. 1977. *Work and family in the United States.* New York: Russell Sage Foundation.

Kanter, Rosabeth Moss. 1977. *Men and women of the corporation.* New York: Basic Books.

Kinsman, Francis. 1987. *The telecommuters.* Chichester, England: Wiley.

Kochan, Thomas A., and Michael Useem. 1992. *Transforming organizations.* New York: Oxford University Press.

Kolb, Deborah M. 1992. Women's work: Peacemaking in organizations. In *Hidden conflict in organizations: Uncovering behind-the-scenes disputes,* ed. Deborah M. Kolb and Jean M. Bartunek. Newbury Park, CA: Sage.

Kunda, Gideon. 1992. *Engineering culture: Control and commitment in a high-tech corporation.* Philadelphia: Temple University Press.

Bibliography

Lobel, Sharon Alisa. 1992. [Special issue on work and family.] *Human Resource Management* 31: 151–265.

Marks, Stephen R. 1977. Multiple roles and role strain: Some notes on human energy, time and commitment. *American Sociological Review* 42: 921–936.

Okin, Susan Moller. 1989. *Justice, gender, and the family*. New York: Basic Books.

Olsen, Frances E. 1983. The family and the market: A study of ideology and legal reform. *Harvard Law Review* 98: 1497–1578.

Perin, Constance. 1991. The moral fabric of the office: Panopticon discourse and schedule flexibilities. In *Research in the sociology of organizations: Organizations and professions*, eds. Pamela S. Tolbert and Stephen R. Barley, 241–268. Greenwich, CT: JAI Press.

Raelin, Joseph A. 1986. *The clash of cultures: Managers and professionals*. Boston: Harvard Business School Press.

Rapoport, Rhona, and Peter Moss. 1990. *Men and women as equals at work: An exploratory study of parental leave in Sweden and career breaks in the U.K.* Thomas Coram Research Unit Occasional Paper No. 11, University of London.

Rodgers, Fran Sussner, and Charles Rodgers. 1989. Business and the facts of family life. *Harvard Business Review* (November-December), 121–129.

Rosenbaum, James E. 1984. *Career mobility in a corporate hierarchy*. Orlando, FL: Academic Press.

Schein, Edgar H. 1992. *Organizational culture and leadership*, 2nd ed. San Francisco: Jossey-Bass.

Schor, Juliet B. 1991. *The overworked American: The unexpected decline of leisure*. New York: Basic Books.

Schwartz, Felice N. (with Jean Zimmerman). 1992. *Breaking with tradition: Women and work, the new facts of life*. New York: Time Warner.

Vanderkolk, Barbara Schwarz, and Arid Armstrong Young. 1991. *The work and family revolution: How companies can keep employees happy and business profitable*. New York: Facts on File.

Bibliography

Van Maanen, John, ed. 1977. *Organizational careers: Some new perspectives*. London: Wiley.

Van Maanen, John, and Gideon Kunda. 1989. "Real feelings": Emotional expression and organizational culture. In *Research in organizational behavior*, vol. 11, eds. Barry M. Staw and Larry L. Cummings. Greenwich, CT: JAI Press.

Wallace, Phyllis A. 1989. *MBAs on the fast track: Career mobility of young managers*. New York: Ballinger.

Williams, Joan C. 1989. Deconstructing gender. *Michigan Law Review* 87: 797–845.

Zedeck, Sheldon. 1992. *Work, families, and organizations*. San Francisco: Jossey-Bass.

Zerubavel, Eviatar. 1981. *Hidden rhythms: Schedules and calendars in social life*. Chicago: University of Chicago Press.

INDEX

Note: Names in quotation marks refer to pseudonyms. *f.* refers to figures, *n.* to notes.

Index

Children, 123–24; *see also* Family
in relation to work, 25, 40,
61–62, 67, 71, 73, 125
Commitment, 69, 104, 105–13;
see also Work involvement
vs. control, 106, 167–68*n*.11
and "Elizabeth Gray," 102,
105, 109, 111
and equity, 112–13
and flexible work conditions,
109, 111
as gauged by visible time, 2–3,
67–68, 81, 106, 110
managerial assumptions about,
105, 106
new way of looking at,
111–12, 126, 127, 136,
137*f*.7–2
and private life, xi, 106–107,
113*f*.6–1
traditional definition of, 106,
110, 112
Communitarian Network
on work and family time,
166*n*.35
Community
involvement with, xi, 150,
162*n*.27
Comparable worth, 115–16, 117
Computer-aided design (CAD),
92–93
Control: *see* Autonomy;
Managerial control; Time
Conway, Elizabeth A.: *see*
Levitan, Sar A.
Cultural assumptions: *see*
Assumptions about work
and careers
Cultural divides, 70, 72*f*.4–1,
122–23; *see also* Boundaries;

Public-private spheres
Customer service, 30, 137,
172–73*n*.24

Delamont, Sara: *see* Atkinson,
Paul
Deming, W. Edwards
on abolishing merit rating, 30
Demographic change, x, 5–6, 39,
65, 152*n*.4
Disaggregation
of tasks from position and pay,
132–33, 172*n*.22
Diversity, 8, 113, 127, 131, 133
of individual needs, 87, 106,
113, 145; *see also* Career orientations
learning from, 127–29, 140,
149–50
of organizational tasks, 87
of work force, 3, 28, 127,
169*n*.
Divorce, 5
effects of, on men and women,
70
Domestic partners
benefits for, 145
Dual careers, 5, 6, 13–25, 41,
45, 125
among academics, 51, 53
Dual ladder, 30–31, 32, 35–36,
133

Empowerment, x, 88, 90, 96
Engineers, 48, 140–41
men vs. women, 48–49
nature of work, 28, 38,
154*n*.6, 158*n*.13
Equal opportunity legislation,
168*n*.13

183

Index

Index

III), 97–104, 105, 106, 109, 111, 121, 122, 123, 132
Gray, Mark" (husband of "Elizabeth Gray"), 98–100

"Hansen, Paul" (venture capitalist), 9–10
Health benefits
inequalities in, 173*n*.10
Hierarchical advancement, 39, 48, 118, 126; *see also* Career success defined as hierarchical advancement
High-commitment organizations, 107, 111–12, 129
Home-based work, 21–22, 66, 86, 94, 106, 137, 145, 149
in Britain, 74
study of, in systems developers, 29, 74, 79–80, 82, 109, 136, 154*n*.5
"Homosocial reproduction," 28, 169*n*.19
Hours of work: *see also* Time
length of, 2, 8, 51–52, 68, 81, 134
as measure of performance, 77, 81, 115
as sign of inefficiency, 77, 81, 82–83, 110, 136
in United States vs. other countries, 68, 84

IBM, 70, 133, 144
and family benefits, 65–66
and relocation, 45
Independent contributors: *see* Careers
Institute for Work Democracy, 114

Intrinsic rewards: *see* Work, rewards of

Japan, 3, 68, 172*n*.22
career paths in, 157*n*.25
and hours of work, 68, 83, 160*n*.16
and organization of work, 68, 122, 171*n*.12
Jobs: *see also* Work
as defined by job holders, 117, 133
"idiosyncratic," 117
measuring value of, 117
psychological demands of, 41, 42
sharing of, 67, 84, 147–48, 149

Kanter, Rosabeth Moss
on absorptiveness of occupational role, 41
on "post-entrepreneurial revolution," 7
Kazarian, Paul B.
ousted from Sunbeam-Oster, 148
Kelly, Lois E.
reaction of, to staff leaves, 142

"Langley, Matthew"
on new approach to work, 124–25
Law
on equal opportunity, 145, 168*n*.13
role of, in change, 78
Leave from work
family and medical, 67
parental, in Sweden, 75–76

Index

Index

Index